Ornamental Designs
from
Architectural Sheet Metal

Ornamental Designs from Architectural Sheet Metal

THE COMPLETE BROSCHART & BRAUN CATALOG, ca. 1900

BROSCHART & BRAUN

A JOINT PUBLICATION OF
THE ATHENAEUM OF PHILADELPHIA AND
DOVER PUBLICATIONS, INC., NEW YORK

Published in Canada by General Publishing Company, Ltd., 30 Lesmill Road, Don Mills, Toronto, Ontario.

Published in the United Kingdom by Constable and Company, Ltd., 3 The Lanchesters, 162–164 Fulham Palace Road, London W6 9ER.

This Athenaeum of Philadelphia/Dover edition, first published in 1992, is an unabridged and unaltered republication of *Artistic Sheet Metal Ornaments*, published by Jacob Broschart & Wm. A. Braun, New York, ca. 1900. A new preface has been written specially for the present edition.

DOVER *Pictorial Archive* SERIES

Manufactured in the United States of America
Dover Publications, Inc., 31 East 2nd Street, Mineola, N.Y. 11501

Library of Congress Cataloging-in-Publication Data

Broschart, Jacob.
    [Artistic sheet metal ornaments]
    Ornamental designs from architectural sheet metal : the complete Broschart & Braun catalog, ca. 1900 / Broschart & Braun [with a new preface].
        p.   cm. — (Dover pictorial archive series)
    "An unabridged and unaltered republication of Artistic sheet metal ornaments"—T.p. verso.
    Includes index.
    ISBN 0-486-27039-4
    1. Broschart & Braun (Firm)—Catalogs.   2. Architectural ironwork—Themes, motives—Catalogs. I. Braun, William A. II. Title. III. Series.
NK8298.B76A4   1992
739.4'77471—dc20
                                                 91-37485
                                                  CIP

Preface to the Athenaeum/Dover Edition

This reprint edition of Jacob Broschart and Wm. A. Braun's *Artistic Sheet Metal Ornaments* is one in a series of reprints of books and trade catalogs published by special agreement between The Athenaeum of Philadelphia and Dover Publications, Inc. The objective of this series is to make available to the greatest possible audience rare and often fragile documents from the extensive collections of The Athenaeum in sturdy and inexpensive editions.

The Athenaeum of Philadelphia is an independent research library with museum collections founded in 1814 to collect materials "connected with the history and antiquities of America, and the useful arts, and generally to disseminate useful knowledge." It is housed in a handsomely restored National Historic Landmark building near Independence Hall in the heart of the historic area of Philadelphia.

As the collections expanded over the past 175 years, The Athenaeum refined its objectives. Today the library concentrates on nineteenth- and early twentieth-century social and cultural history, particularly architecture and interior design where the collections are nationally significant. The library is freely open to serious investigators, and it annually attracts thousands of readers: graduate students and senior scholars, architects, interior designers, museum curators and private owners of historic houses.

In addition to 130,000 architectural drawings, 25,000 historic photographs and several million manuscripts, The Athenaeum's library is particularly rich in original works on architecture, interior design and domestic technology. In the latter area the publications of manufacturers and dealers in architectural elements and interior embellishments have been found to be particularly useful to design professionals and historic house owners who are concerned with the restoration or the recreation of period interiors. Consequently, many of the reprints in this series are drawn from this collection. The Athenaeum's holdings are particularly strong in areas such as paint colors, lighting fixtures, wallpaper, heating and kitchen equipment, plumbing and household furniture.

The modern Athenaeum also sponsors a diverse program of lectures, chamber music concerts and exhibitions. It publishes books that reflect the institution's collecting interests, and it administers several trusts that provide awards and research grants to recognize literary achievement and to encourage outstanding scholarship in architectural history throughout the United States. For further information, write The Athenaeum of Philadelphia, East Washington Square, Philadelphia, PA 19106-3794.

ROGER W. MOSS
EXECUTIVE DIRECTOR

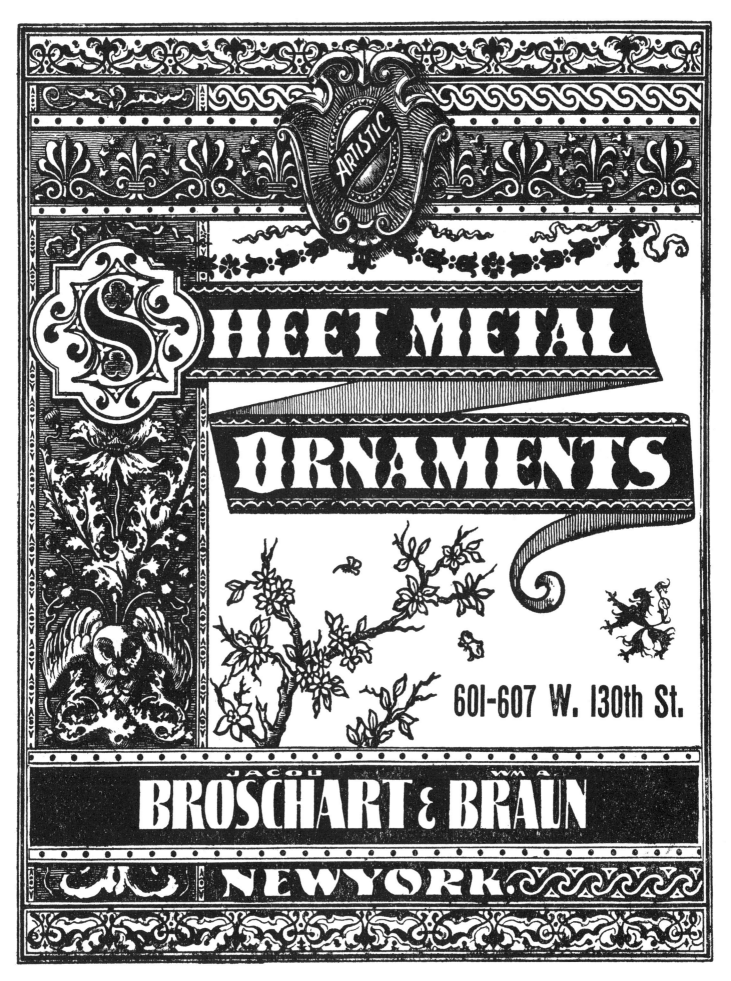

SHEET METAL ORNAMENTS

601-607 W. 130th St.

JACOB BROSCHART & BRAUN WM A

NEW YORK.

[Original front cover]

PLEASE NOTICE THAT

All Illustrations shown in this Catalógue are ONE-EIGHTH the actual size.

IN offering this new Catalogue Edition of   .   .   .

High Grade Architectural Sheet Metal Ornaments manufactured by us, we trust that if you have not as yet used any of our goods, you will give them a trial at your first opportunity. We are satisfied that their superiority of workmanship, combined with reasonable prices, will earn us your future and constant patronage.

With a carefully selected plant of the latest improved machinery and an expert force of skilled artisans, we are enabled to keep a large stock of these designs on hand and to furnish any quantity at short notice.

Making a specialty of carrying out Architects' **Original Designs**, we will be pleased to submit estimates for such work.

Prices quoted in this catalogue are for **Zinc**. Prices for **Copper** will be furnished on application.

Yours very truly,

BROSCHART & BRAUN.

DON'T cut out these illustrations, but ORDER BY NUMBER.

When ordering goods, please state if they are to be shipped by FREIGHT OR EXPRESS.

The designs in this catalogue are only a few of the many we carry in stock. If they do not fill your wants, please send tracings.

NOTICE.—Unless otherwise expressly ordered, and agreed, all goods are shipped **IN PARTS** and nested, to avoid bulk and prevent damage in transit. Extra charge will be made for goods put together and soldered, complete; also for package.

INDEX

PAGE

	PAGE
Angles Leaves,	73
Balls,	76
Balusters,	75, 77
Bead Enrichments,	20, 21
Brackets,	5, 6, 7, 8
Bracket Fronts,	9, 10, 11, 12
Bracket Leaves,	9, 10, 11, 12
Bracket Rolls,	10
Capitals,	54, 55, 56, 57, 58
Cartouches,	51, 52
Centre Pieces,	44, 45, 46, 47, 48
Cheneau,	67, 68, 69, 70, 71, 72
Corbels,	8, 9
Cresting,	67, 68, 69, 70, 71, 72
Crockets,	58
Curved Enrichment,	18, 19, 20
Dental Frieze,	26
Drapery,	17, 22, 23
Drop Ornaments,	40, 41
Eagles,	49, 50
Egg and Dart Enrichments,	15, 16
Enrichments, 15, 16, 17, 18, 19, 20, 21, 22, 23, 24, 25, 26, 27
Faces,	48, 49, 50, 51
Festoons,	36, 37, 38, 39, 40
Finials,	58, 59, 60, 61, 62, 63, 64, 65
Fish Scales, (Schuppen),	10
Flames,	60, 61
Fleur de lis,	21, 23, 24
Flute Enrichment,	26, 27
Foot Leaves,	8, 9
Frieze,	21, 22, 23, 24, 25, 26, 27
Gargoyles,	50

	PAGE
Garlands,	36, 37, 38, 39, 40
Heads,	48, 49, 50, 51
Leader Straps,	27, 28
Leaves,	9, 10, 11, 12
Letters,	74
Lion Heads,	48, 49
Modillions,	5, 6, 7, 8
Numbers,	74
Ogee Enrichment,	17, 18
Panels,	30, 31, 32, 33, 34, 35, 36
Panel Ornaments,	12, 13, 14, 15, 27, 28, 29
Pendants,	59, 60, 61
Pinacles,	59, 60, 61
Ribbons,	41, 42
Rock Face,	74, 75
Rope Enrichment,	18, 19
Rosettes,	44, 45, 46, 47, 48
Scrolls,	12, 13, 14, 15
Shells,	53, 54
Shields,	51, 52
Shingles,	74
Soffit Rosettes,	46, 47
Sun-bursts,	53, 54
Tiles,	74
Tower,	75
Truss Front, (Schuppen),	10
Tympanums,	30, 31, 32, 33, 34, 35
Urns,	66
Vases,	66
Volutes,	73
Weather Vanes,	62, 63, 64, 65
Wreaths,	42, 43

INDEX AND TELEGRAPHIC CIPHER.

No.	Cipher	Page	No.	Cipher	Page	No.	Cipher	Page	No.	Cipher	Page	No.	Cipher	Page	No.	Cipher	Page
3	Aback	7	144	Ariel	6	224	Aggrieve	5	340	Allegro	11	464	Analepsis	12	723	Blot	14
6	Abaft	8	145	Affable	6	225	Aghast	5	341	Alleluiah	11	501	Argue	10	724	Bedouin	14
7	Abattis	6	146	Affair	6	226	Agile	6	342	Allemande	12	506	Arouse	10	725	Blow	13
11	Abash	7	147	Affirm	6	228	Agnate	5	343	Alleviate	12	507	Arrant	10	726	Bluff	14
18	Abate	6	148	Afflict	6	229	Agnomen	6	345	Alliance	11	508	Arrange	10	727	Blunt	13
19	Abet	6	149	Affray	6	230	Agnostic	6	346	Alligator	11	509	Array	10	728	Bode	12
20	Abject	5	150	Affront	6	232	Ago	8	350	Alone	10	510	Artless	10	729	Bodily	12
28	Abjure	5	153	Adjunct	5	233	Agoing	5	352	Also	9	511	Assent	10	730	Bowlder	12
37	Abound	6	154	Adjure	6	234	Agrarian	5	367	Alter	9	512	Ask	10	731	Beeswax	14
38	About	5	155	Adjust	8	235	Aggressor	7	368	Always	9	513	Assemble	10	732	Bold	12
42	Abrupt	5	156	Adjutant	5	269	Alabaster	6	379	Amazed	10	514	Assign	10	733	Booty	12
45	Abscond	5	162	Ado	5	301	Afraid	9	380	Amend	10	515	Assert	10	734	Bore	13
46	Absent	5	164	Adolescent	5	302	Age	9	381	Ample	10	516	Assume	10	735	Beefsteak	13
47	Absolve	5	165	Adoption	6	303	Agency	9	382	Amuse	10	517	Assist	10	736	Beer	15
55	Abstain	5	166	Adorable	6	304	Aged	9	383	Analogy	10	518	Athletic	10	737	Beet	15
56	Abstruse	5	168	Adornment	5	305	Agitate	9	384	Ancient	10	519	Attach	10	739	Beggar	13
58	Abuse	6	170	Adrift	8	307	Alguazil	11	386	Anger	9	520	Attend	10	740	Border	13
67	Accede	7	172	Adulation	6	308	Alias	11	387	Angry	9	521	Attire	10	741	Begonia	13
70	Accept	7	176	Adust	5	309	Agony	9	389	Annual	10	522	August	10	742	Branch	12
71	Access	5	177	Advance	5	310	Agonize	10	390	Annex	10	523	Avail	10	746	Brand	12
77	Accrue	6	178	Advantage	6	311	Alibi	10	391	Althorn	11	524	Avow	10	748	Brave	12
78	Accord	6	180	Adventure	6	312	Ailing	9	392	Although	12	525	Awaken	10	749	Break	12
79	Accost	6	183	Advertise	7	315	Align	11	393	Altimeter	11	526	Awry	10	751	Brief	13
90	Accuse	7	186	Advow	6	316	Aid	10	394	Altitude	11	527	Bad	10	752	Bright	12
95	Achieve	6	187	Adze	5	317	Aim	10	424	Announce	9	528	Balmy	10	753	Brisk	12
104	Acquaint	8	188	Afar	6	318	Aliment	11	427	Annoy	9	529	Baffle	10	754	Broad	13
119	Acquit	6	190	Affected	6	319	Air	9	431	Annul	9	530	Barely	10	755	Bellicose	13
120	Act	6	191	Aeolian	6	320	Alarm	9	432	Anxiety	9	531	Bargain	10	756	Bruise	14
121	Action	6	192	Aeon	6	321	Alimony	11	437	Appeal	9	701	Battle	13	757	Brutal	12
122	Actor	5	193	Affiance	6	322	Alike	10	438	Appoint	9	703	Base	13	758	Built	15
123	Adage	7	194	Affidavit	6	324	Alert	10	439	Apt	10	705	Beating	12	759	Burden	13
124	Adapt	7	198	Aerate	6	325	Alive	10	440	Amiss	10	706	Beastly	12	760	Burial	12
126	Add	7	199	Affix	5	326	All	9	441	Amity	10	707	Beatify	13	761	Burst	12
127	Adept	5	202	Afford	8	328	Allay	9	442	Ammonia	10	708	Beatitude	14	762	Bury	14
131	Adieu	6	203	Affright	6	329	Allege	9	443	Ammunition	10	710	Bare	12	763	But	15
132	Adjourn	6	206	Afire	5	330	Albert	11	444	Amnesty	10	711	Bean	12	764	Buy	12
134	Adjust	6	209	Afoot	8	331	Allow	9	445	Among	10	712	Beguile	13	765	Belt	13
135	Adopt	7	212	Africa	6	332	Allude	9	448	Amount	11	713	Blame	12	766	Bench	13
137	Admire	8	213	Aft	6	334	Allure	9	450	Amphibious	11	714	Blast	12	769	Benediction	13
138	Admit	8	215	Afterward	8	335	Allah	11	451	Amphora	9	716	Beaver	14	771	Benefice	13
140	Adore	7	216	Again	8	336	Allspice	11	452	Amplitude	9	717	Becalm	14	772	Benefit	14
141	Adroit	6	217	Agape	8	337	Allegiance	11	453	Amputate	11	718	Blend	12	774	Bengal	13
142	Adverse	7	220	Agent	8	338	Almighty	10	454	Amuck	11	719	Becket	14	901	Cabal	9
143	Advice	6	223	Aggress	5	339	Allegory	11	463	Analysis	10	721	Blind	15	902	Call	9

INDEX AND TELEGRAPHIC CIPHER

No.	Cipher	Page
904	Callous	9
906	Cancel	8
907	Canvas	8
908	Care	8
910	Carol	8
911	Carry	8
912	Cabas	8
913	Cabbage	8
914	Cabin	8
916	Cable	9
920	Cachalot	8
921	Cache	9
922	Cachou	8
925	Cacophony	8
926	Cactus	8
927	Cad	8
928	Cadaverous	8
1102	Case	16
1103	Cash	16
1104	Cast	16
1105	Catch	16
1106	Cause	16
1108	Cede	16
1110	Caravan	16
1112	Certain	15
1113	Certify	16
1114	Chance	15
1115	Chaff	16
1116	Change	15
1117	Charge	16
1121	Charity	15
1131	Charm	16
1134	Chary	16
1135	Chasten	15
1136	Chat	16
1137	Cheat	16
1138	Cheer	16
1139	Check	16
1140	Chief	16
1141	Choice	16
1142	Choose	16
1143	Cardiac	16
1144	Cartioid	15
1145	Cardinal	16
1146	Cardoon	15
1147	Careful	16
1148	Career	16
1149	Caress	16
1150	Caret	16
1151	Cargo	16
1152	Caribou	15
1154	Caries	16
1155	Carinate	15
1157	Carl	16
1158	Carline	16
1159	Carmelite	16
1160	Carminitive	15
1161	Carmine	16
1162	Carnage	16
1163	Carnival	16
1164	Carnal	16
1165	Carob	16
1166	Carotid	16
1401	Civil	17
1402	Clamor	17
1403	Clear	17
1404	Clever	17
1405	Climb	17
1406	Cling	17
1408	Cloak	17
1409	Close	17
1410	Cloudy	17
1411	Clutch	17
1412	Coarse	17
1413	Commerce	17
1414	Commit	17
1415	Companion	17
1416	Compel	17
1417	Company	17
1418	Complex	17
1419	Compound	17
1423	Comprise	18
1424	Comrade	17
1427	Conceal	17
1429	Concede	18
1431	Concert	17
1432	Concise	17
1433	Condemn	17
1435	Chapellet	17
1446	Confess	17
1447	Confound	17
1448	Confront	17
1449	Conjure	17
1450	Connect	17
1451	Conquer	17
1452	Console	17
1453	Constant	17
1454	Construct	17
1456	Consume	17
1457	Contain	17
1459	Charles	18
1460	Content	17
1461	Charmer	18
1462	Charing	18
1463	Charnal	18
1464	Chart	18
1465	Charter	18
1466	Chartist	18
1467	Chartreuse	18
1468	Chase	18
1469	Chasm	18
1470	Chassepot	18
1471	Chasseur	18
1472	Chaste	18
1473	Chastize	18
1474	Chasuble	18
1476	Chateau	18
1477	Chatoyant	18
1478	Chattel	18
1479	Chavinism	18
1480	Cheddar	18
1481	Cheek	18
1605	Contest	19
1606	Contract	19
1607	Control	19
1608	Converse	19
1609	Convey	19
1610	Convert	20
1611	Cool	20
1612	Copy	19
1613	Cordial	19
1614	Correct	19
1615	Counsel	20
1617	Couple	19
1619	Cist	19
1620	Courage	20
1622	Courtesy	19
1623	Crafty	19
1624	Crave	19
1625	Crazy	19
1626	Crest	19
1627	Crude	19
1628	Cite	19
1629	Citation	20
1630	Cithern	19
1631	Citron	19
1632	Citrate	18
1634	Citadel	19
1635	Citizen	20
1636	Civic	19
1637	Civilian	19
1638	Civilize	19
1904	Crew	21
1905	Crime	20
1906	Cross	20
1907	Cruel	21
1908	Curb	20
1909	Curtail	20
1910	Custody	20
1911	Custom	20
1916	Culminate	20
1917	Cut	20
1920	Dally	20
1924	Damp	20
1925	Damage	20
1941	Danger	20
1942	Dare	20
1943	Dash	20
1945	Date	20
1946	Daunt	20
1947	Dead	20
1949	Dame	20
1951	Damson	21
1952	Dance	20
1954	Dandle	20
1955	Daphne	20
1956	Dapper	20
1957	Dapple	20
1958	Dark	20
1959	Darksome	20
1960	Darn	20
1961	Darnex	21
2201	Dawn	22
2202	Dear	22
2203	Debate	22
2204	Decay	22
2205	Deceit	22
2206	Decent	22
2207	Decide	22
2208	Declare	22
2209	Decoy	21
2210	Decry	21
2211	Deem	21
2212	Deep	21
2213	Deface	21
2215	Defame	23
2216	Default	23
2217	Defeat	25
2219	Defect	24
2220	Defray	25
2222	Degree	25
2223	Delight	22
2224	Deny	22
2226	Depart	21
2233	Deprive	21
2235	Depute	21
2236	Desert	21
2237	Design	23
2239	Deserve	25
2243	Depicture	22
2244	Depilatory	23
2245	Deplete	24
2247	Desist	25
2248	Despair	24
2249	Detail	23
2250	Detect	23
2255	Deter	63
2256	Depolarize	22
2257	Devoid	22
2258	Depone	22
2260	Deport	22
2261	Deportment	22
2262	Depose	22
2263	Deposable	21
2264	Deposal	23
2265	Deposit	22
2266	Depositor	22
2267	Depot	22
2268	Deprave	21
2269	Depravity	22
2270	Deprecate	22
2271	Depreciate	24
2274	Depression	22
2275	Depressor	25
2276	Depurate	22
2278	Deputy	24
2279	Derange	24
2289	Dermalgia	21
2401	Dextrous	28
2402	Diabetes	29
2403	Device	27
2404	Dictate	27
2406	Diacritic	28
2407	Die	27
2408	Dire	28
2410	Direct	28
2411	Diagnosis	29
2412	Diagonal	28
2413	Diagram	29
2414	Dial	28
2415	Dialect	29
2416	Dialogue	29
2418	Disclose	27
2422	Disgrace	27
2424	Disguise	41
2429	Dismal	28
2432	Disown	28
2434	Display	15
2435	Dispute	28
2436	Distant	28
2437	Distinct	28
2439	Distrust	28
2440	Disturb	27
2441	Dogmatic	27
2442	Dickey	29
2444	Dictator	28
2445	Dictum	27
2446	Divine	40
2447	Divide	27
2448	Dimple	27
2449	Dodge	28
2450	Dove	28
2451	Doing	28
2452	Dictionary	29
2453	Didactic	28
2459	Dietary	28
2462	Difference	29
2463	Difficult	29
2464	Diffident	27
2466	Diffract	27
2467	Diffuse	28
2468	Diffusion	28
2469	Dig	28
2470	Digger	29
2472	Digastric	28
2474	Digestible	29
2475	Digestion	29
2476	Digestive	29
2477	Dight	29
2478	Digit	28
2479	Digital	28
2480	Digitate	29
2481	Dignify	29
2482	Dignity	28
2486	Digression	28
2601	Doom	21
2602	Doubt	21
2603	Dread	21
2604	Dress	21
2608	Disperse	23
2610	Displace	21
2611	Disport	21
2612	Dispose	23
2703	Dream	19
2704	Drill	19
2705	Drive	19
2706	Drool	19
2707	Dunce	19
2708	Dwell	19
2709	Eager	19
2711	Earring	18
2712	Earldom	18
2713	Early	18
2714	Earnest	19
2801	Earn	27
2802	Ease	26
2804	Eclipse	26
2805	Edge	26
2807	Efface	26
2808	Effect	26
2809	Effuse	26
2810	Embrace	26
2811	Effusion	27
2812	Effusive	26
2813	Enclose	26
2814	End	26
2815	Egg	26
2817	Eggplant	26
2818	Eglantine	27
2819	Egoism	27
2820	Egotistic	26
2821	Endless	26
2822	Egregious	26
2823	Egress	26
2824	Egression	26
2825	Egret	26
2826	Egypt	26
2827	Eiderdown	26
2828	Eiderduck	26
2829	Eidograph	26
2831	Ejection	26
2832	Ejectment	27
2833	Ejector	27
2834	Elaborate	27
2836	Elaine	27
2837	Eland	26
2839	Elastic	26
2841	Elate	26
3001	Emulsive	35
3002	Endure	30
3004	Energy	35
3005	Engross	35
3006	Engulf	34
3007	Enlarge	30
3008	Enlighten	30
3009	Enmity	30
3010	Enough	30
3011	Enact	34
3013	Entrance	30
3014	Entreat	31
3017	Envy	35
3019	Equal	32
3020	Estate	33
3021	Esteem	30
3022	Event	35
3023	Ever	30
3024	Evil	33
3025	Evince	33
3026	Exceed	31
3027	Excel	31
3028	Except	31
3029	Excuse	31
3030	Exhaust	35
3031	Exist	35
3032	Exile	35
3034	Enameler	15
3035	Enamor	32
3037	Encamp	31
3038	Encampment	31
3039	Encaustic	32
3041	Enchant	34
3043	Enchantment	31
3044	Enchase	32
3045	Enchorial	32
3046	Encircle	30
3047	Enclave	30
3048	Enclitic	30
3049	Enconium	31
3050	Encompass	34
3051	Encore	36
3052	Encounter	32
3053	Encourage	32
3054	Encrinite	32
3055	Encroach	30
3056	Encrocher	30
3057	Encumber	30
3058	Encyclical	30
3059	Encysted	33
3060	Ending	35
3061	Endlessly	33
3062	Endanger	34
3063	Endear	34
3064	Endearment	34
3065	Endeavor	36
3066	Endecagon	32
3201	Expand	37
3202	Expect	37
3203	Expel	37
3204	Eternal	38
3205	Estuary	38
3206	Expert	36
3208	Expire	36
3209	Evident	39
3210	Explore	38
3211	Express	39
3212	Extend	38
3213	Extol	36
3216	Examine	36
3217	Exemplary	39
3219	Excellent	37
3220	Extort	37
3221	Extract	38
3223	Face	39
3224	Fame	39
3226	Fancy	37
3227	Farthest	38
3228	Fashion	39
3229	Fatal	38
3237	Favor	37
3239	Fearless	37
3240	Fearful	37
3242	Feeling	37
3243	Feign	37
3244	Felicity	40
3245	Fertile	36
3246	Festal	36
3247	Feud	36
3248	Fickle	36
3249	Fiction	36
3250	Fierce	36
3251	Fight	36
3252	Figure	36
3253	Fill	36
3254	Final	36
3255	Finish	37
3257	Factious	36
3258	First	37
3261	Firm	38
3262	Firmer	38
3263	Fitful	38
3264	Fix	38
3265	Flat	36
3266	Fleeting	36
3267	Faculty	37
3268	Fadeless	37
3269	Fagot	37
3271	Fair	40
3272	Fairly	38
3274	Fairy	39
3275	Fay	37
3276	Faith	37
3277	Faithful	37
3279	Falcon	39
3280	Falconet	39
3281	Faldstool	39
3282	Fallow	39
3283	Fanny	39
3284	Famous	39
3285	Family	39
3286	Familiar	39
3287	Fanatic	39
3288	Farina	39
3289	Farm	38
3290	Faro	38
3291	Farrier	38
3292	Farthing	38
3295	Fascinate	37
3296	Fast	37
3297	Fastday	37
3298	Fastidious	37
3299	Fatten	37
3300	Fate	37
3301	Fatalism	37
3302	Father	37
3303	Fathom	37
3304	Fatigue	37
3305	Fatuous	37
3306	Faubourg	37
3307	Faucet	36
3402	Flight	40
3403	Flimsy	40
3404	Fling	40
3405	Flood	41
3406	Flavor	41
3407	Flax	41
3408	Flesh	37
3409	Flexible	41
3411	Fluent	41
3412	Fluster	41
3413	Foe	27
3416	Fold	41
3417	Follow	41
3418	Folly	41
3419	Footing	41
3421	Floral	41
3422	Forbid	41
3423	Foreign	41
3424	Form	40
3425	Formal	41
3426	Forward	28
3427	Foul	41
3428	Free	27
3432	Flounder	41
3433	Flour	41
3434	Flow	41
3602	Fresh	48
3603	Fretful	48
3604	Fright	48
3605	Front	48
3607	Frugal	48
3610	Fulfil	48
3612	Gale	48
3613	Gallant	48
3614	Gabion	45
3615	Gage	45
3616	Gaudy	48
3617	Gaunt	48
3619	Gay	48
3621	Genial	48
3622	Genteel	48
3626	Gentle	48
3627	Gesture	48
3628	Ghost	48
3631	Gibe	47
3632	Giddy	47
3633	Gift	48
3634	Gird	47
3635	Girdle	48
3636	Give	48
3639	Glad	48
3640	Glitter	48
3645	Gloom	44
3646	Godly	44
3650	Grand	44
3651	Good	44
3654	Grace	44
3655	Grade	44
3656	Ground	44
3657	Group	44
3658	Grow	44
3659	Grudge	44
3661	Gruff	44
3662	Guard	44
3663	Guess	44
3665	Guide	44
3667	Greyhound	44
3668	Guise	44
3669	Halt	44
3673	Hand	44
3674	Happy	44
3676	Handle	44
3678	Harass	44
3680	Harm	44
3681	Harsh	44
3682	Hasten	44
3683	Hasty	47
3685	Hate	44
3686	Havoc	44
3688	Hazard	44
3690	Heal	44
3691	Healthy	45
3693	Hear	44
3694	Help	44
3695	Hidden	45
3697	High	45
3699	Hint	45
3700	Hire	45
3701	Honest	45
3703	Hammer	45
3712	Hope	44
3713	Horror	44
3715	Hoist	48
3726	Horse	45
3729	Huge	44
3730	Humane	44
3733	Humble	44
3746	Humor	45
3749	Humbly	48
3750	Hurl	46
3751	Hurry	45
3752	Hurtful	45
3753	Hump	44
3754	Illegal	46
3755	Illume	44
3756	Illness	44
3757	Image	45
3758	Imagine	48
3759	Imbibe	44
3760	Immense	44
3761	Immure	46
3762	Impart	47
3763	Imp	48
3765	Impel	47
3767	Imposing	46
3769	Include	44
3770	Increase	46
3771	Indicate	46
3772	Induce	46
3775	Inert	47
3776	Infect	47
3778	Infirm	47
3781	Inflame	47

INDEX AND TELEGRAPHIC CIPHER.

No.	Cipher	Page
3782	Inform	47
3785	Inhuman	44
3786	Injustice	44
3791	Inflexible	44
3793	Infringe	47
3795	Inquiry	44
3796	Instigate	44
3797	Interdict	44
3798	Invaluable	44
3799	Infuse	47
3800	Inscribe	47
3801	Inside	47
3802	Insipid	47
3803	Insist	46
3804	Ingrain	48
3814	Infinite	45
3815	Informal	47
3816	Intact	47
3818	Intrepid	44
3819	Inca	48
3820	Incentive	44
3823	Incident	47
3824	Index	45
3825	Indian	48
3826	Indict	44
3827	Ineffable	44
3828	Ingenious	44
3833	Ingot	44
3835	Ingrained	44
3836	Inhabit	44
3837	Inherit	48
3838	Inlay	44
3840	Innocent	44
3842	Innovate	47
3845	Inroad	45
3846	Insight	44
3847	Insignia	45
3848	Inspire	48
3849	Instal	45
3850	Instant	47
3851	Institute	48
3854	Insular	44
3856	Insure	45
3858	Intercede	47
3859	Interlude	44
3860	Intone	44
4001	Inspect	41
4002	Intrench	42
4004	Invade	41
4007	Insnare	41
4011	Instill	41
4012	Instruct	42
4013	Intellect	42
4014	Integrity	41
4015	Intend	41
4016	Interest	42
4017	Interior	42
4019	Intimacy	42
4028	Intimate	42
4030	Intrigue	42
4031	Invincible	42
4034	Invoke	41
4035	Iodine	42
4036	Island	41
4037	Isolate	42
4038	Incast	42
4039	Indigo	42
4040	Isthmus	42
4041	Insurance	42
4042	Inject	42
4044	Ivory	41
4201	Intrinsic	43
4202	Intrude	43
4203	Intrust	43
4206	Invent	42
4209	Invert	42
4210	Ivy	43
4212	Involve	43
4214	Inward	42
4215	Italy	43
4216	Irony	42
4217	Issue	42
4218	Ireland	43
4220	Islam	43
4221	Isinglass	43
4222	Irruption	43
4223	Iota	42
4224	Invite	43
4225	Inventor	42
4226	Invest	43
4227	Invasion	43
4402	Judgment	49
4404	Jacinth	49
4407	Justify	49
4408	Junction	49
4409	Justness	49
4411	Jut	48
4412	Japan	49
4413	Keen	49
4414	Keep	48
4415	Key	48
4416	Kill	48

No.	Cipher	Page
4418	Kaolin	49
4419	Kind	48
4420	Kindred	48
4421	Labor	48
4422	Lame	48
4425	Lament	49
4429	Label	49
4430	Language	50
4431	Lace	49
4432	Languid	48
4433	Laconic	51
4434	Lacrosse	50
4442	Large	50
4443	Ladder	50
4444	Last	50
4445	Lasting	50
4447	Laud	49
4448	Lazy	49
4449	Leader	49
4450	Led	49
4451	Lagoon	49
4453	Lean	48
4454	Leap	50
4455	Learn	49
4456	Legend	49
4457	Lamb	50
4458	Lampoon	49
4460	Lance	49
4463	Landlord	51
4466	Landau	48
4467	Lantern	49
4468	Lanyard	49
4470	Lapwing	49
4471	Larboard	50
4472	Lark	50
4473	Lasso	51
4474	Lath	50
4475	Latitude	50
4602	Launch	53
4603	Lawful	54
4604	Level	54
4605	Lawn	54
4606	League	54
4607	Leather	53
4608	Ledger	54
4609	Legacy	54
4610	Levity	53
4611	Legion	53
4612	Legislate	54
4615	Liable	53
4616	Liberal	54
4617	Lie	53
4618	Life	53
4619	Light	53
4620	Likeness	53
4622	Limit	53
4626	Lineage	53
4631	Listen	53
4633	List	53
4634	Listless	53
4635	Little	53
4636	Live	53
4637	Lively	53
4638	Loose	53
4639	Loss	53
4640	Lot	53
4641	Legate	54
4646	Loud	53
4647	Love	53
4648	Mad	54
4649	Maintain	53
4650	Majestic	53
4654	Make	53
4655	Machine	54
4656	Mackerel	54
4658	Madam	54
4660	Magazine	53
4661	Magnate	54
4801	Malady	55
4802	Magenta	54
4803	Malice	55
4804	Manager	55
4805	Magnesia	56
4806	Magnet	56
4807	Magnolia	54
4808	Magnetic	58
4809	Mangle	55
4810	Mahogany	54
4811	Mania	55
4812	Maiden	54
4813	Mail	54
4814	Manifest	57
4815	Manifold	57
4816	Majolica	54
4817	Major	54
4818	Manly	55
4819	Manner	57
4820	Malachite	54
4821	Margin	56
4822	Malaga	54
4824	Mark	55
4825	Massive	55

No.	Cipher	Page
4826	Master	55
4827	Mallet	55
4829	Matchless	54
4830	Mamma	55
4832	Mammoth	55
4833	Mammon	55
4834	Mankind	55
4835	Matrimony	55
4836	Matter	55
4837	Mature	56
4838	Maudlin	55
4839	Mawkish	55
4840	Maybe	55
4841	Meagre	55
4842	Mean	55
4843	Meaning	56
4845	Memory	55
4847	Menace	55
4848	Mend	56
4849	Menial	55
4850	Mental	55
4851	Mandarin	56
4855	Mandamus	55
4856	Mandate	56
4859	Mandatory	54
4860	Mandrake	57
4862	Manger	57
4863	Mango	55
4864	Mangrove	55
4865	Manor	56
4866	Mantel	56
4867	Mantua	56
4868	Manual	56
4869	Manumit	54
4870	Maple	56
4871	Marble	56
4872	Marigold	55
4875	Maritime	57
4876	Marjoram	57
4878	Market	56
4880	Marmalade	55
4881	Marmot	55
4882	Maroon	55
4884	Martial	54
4885	Marshal	55
4886	Martello	57
4887	Martinet	55
4888	Mastiff	55
4892	Mastadon	58
4893	Matress	55
4894	Maxim	57
4895	Mediate	58
4896	Meditate	57
4897	Medium	58
4899	Mellow	58
4900	Melody	57
4901	Mention	55
4906	Membrane	57
4907	Memoir	58
4909	Memento	57
4910	Mendicant	58
4911	Mentor	58
4912	Mercury	57
4913	Monkey	58
4915	Merino	57
4916	Mermaid	57
5001	Merchant	60
5002	Merciful	60
5003	Messmate	61
5004	Metaphor	59
5005	Meteor	58
5006	Merry	60
5007	Mercy	60
5008	Method	60
5011	Mighty	60
5012	Mild	60
5014	Mind	60
5015	Mingle	60
5016	Minute	59
5017	Minister	60
5018	Mica	61
5019	Midland	61
5021	Miscreant	60
5023	Microbe	58
5024	Mignon	58
5025	Miserly	58
5026	Misguide	58
5029	Mikado	60
5035	Migrate	61
5039	Mineral	66
5041	Mistake	66
5042	Misty	66
5043	Minnow	66
5044	Minuet	66
5045	Minstrel	59
5046	Mint	59
5047	Miracle	59
5048	Mirror	58
5051	Missal	58
5052	Mission	58
5055	Mobile	60
5056	Moccasin	61

No.	Cipher	Page
5057	Mocha	58
5059	Mistigate	60
5060	Mix	60
5061	Mob	60
5062	Modern	58
5064	Mogul	58
5065	Mohair	58
5072	Mahomet	60
5073	Molar	58
5074	Molecule	59
5075	Monad	58
5076	Monarch	58
5077	Monastic	58
5078	Monogram	58
5080	Monopoly	60
5081	Monitor	61
5082	Monsoon	60
5083	Moon	58
5084	Morass	60
5086	Morocco	58
5089	Morceau	60
5090	Morion	60
5092	Mormon	60
5093	Mortar	59
5094	Moslem	58
5095	Mossrose	61
5096	Motto	60
5098	Mound	58
5099	Mountain	58
5100	Motor	58
5101	Mulatto	52
5102	Mulberry	52
5104	Mode	52
5106	Moderate	52
5107	Moreover	52
5108	Mule	52
5109	Morn	52
5112	Morose	52
5113	Mummy	51
5114	Morify	51
5115	Most	52
5116	Motive	51
5117	Mould	52
5119	Mundane	52
5123	Mungo	52
5124	Mural	52
5125	Muriate	52
5127	Muscle	52
5128	Muscovy	52
5129	Mushroom	52
5130	Musician	52
5131	Museum	52
5201	Mount	68
5202	Mourn	67
5203	More	67
5204	Mush	67
5205	Murmur	67
5206	Muster	68
5207	Mutable	68
5208	Mutinous	67
5209	Name	67
5210	Narrow	67
5211	Nabob	77
5212	Nation	67
5214	Naiad	72
5215	Native	67
5218	Natural	67
5219	Nainsook	70
5222	Naptha	71
5223	Napkin	69
5224	Narcissus	69
5226	Narcotic	70
5227	Naval	72
5228	Nazarene	69
5229	Neat	68
5230	Nebnla	68
5231	Nectar	70
5232	Needle	68
5233	Neutral	71
5234	Neptune	68
5235	Nervine	69
5236	Nestor	71
5237	Nicotine	69
5238	Noble	69
5239	Nomad	72
5240	Nominee	68
5241	Nonpareil	72
5243	Noontide	68
5244	Normal	68
5245	Notary	70
5246	Novel	69
5401	Neat	73
5402	Novelty	73
5403	Need	73
5405	Novice	73
5407	Needy	73
5408	Nerve	73
5412	Nucleus	73
5413	Nettle	73
5416	Nigh	73
5419	Nimble	73
5420	Noise	73

No.	Cipher	Page
5424	Notable	73
5425	Note	73
5226	Nugget	73
5427	Notify	73
5429	Notice	73
5430	Notion	73
5431	Obedient	73
5432	Oak	73
5433	Object	73
5434	Oblige	73
5436	Obscure	73
5437	Observe	73
5438	Obsolete	73
5439	Obvious	73
5440	Occasion	73
5441	Occur	73
5442	Oasis	73
5443	Obelisk	73
5444	Obligate	73
5445	Obstinate	73
5461	Occupy	73
5463	Occupant	73
5464	Ocean	73
5469	Ocelot	73
5470	Ochre	73
5471	Octoroon	73
5472	Ocular	73
5473	Offspring	73
5491	Official	73
5501	Occult	10
5502	Odd	10
5507	Odor	10
5508	Offence	10
5509	Offhand	10
5510	Offend	10
5511	Office	10
5512	Officer	10
5513	Omission	10
5514	Omen	10
5701	Omnipotent	65
5703	Oust	62
5704	Oleander	65
5705	Open	64
5706	Oppose	64
5707	Oration	60
5708	Option	65
5710	Ordain	66
5711	Oligarch	62
5718	Ordinary	64
5720	Origin	62
5721	Outcast	63
5722	Outcry	63
5723	Outdo	62
5724	Outline	61
5725	Outrage	63
5726	Outward	65
5727	Overcome	64
5728	Overjoyed	63
5729	Oversee	60
5730	Outside	64
5732	Outing	64
5733	Oversight	65
5734	Olympus	63
5735	Omnibus	62
5737	Omega	65
5738	Omelet	63
5739	Omniform	62
5740	Onset	61
5741	Onyx	66
5742	Opal	61
5743	Opaque	61
5744	Opera	61
5745	Opportune	61
5746	Oppress	64
5747	Oppugn	62
5748	Optative	63
5749	Optic	66
5750	Optician	59
5751	Opulent	61
5752	Ormolu	61
5754	Oracle	61
5755	Orator	66
5757	Orison	58
5758	Orange	59
5759	Orchard	66
5761	Orchestra	66
5762	Orchid	59
5763	Ordeal	66
5801	Ordain	74
5806	Ordinate	75
5807	Organic	75
5815	Oriental	74
5816	Oriole	75
5914	Orion	74
5915	Orleans	74
5916	Orphan	74
5917	Orphean	74
5918	Orthodox	74
5919	Ortolan	74
5920	Oscillate	74
5921	Ospray	74
5922	Ostrich	74

No.	Cipher	Page
5923	Ottoman	74
5925	Outwardly	75
5929	Outbreak	74
5930	Outfit	74
5931	Outlaw	74
5932	Outwork	74
5933	Ovation	74
5934	Oven	74
5935	Overcast	74
5936	Overflow	74
6001	Pay	77
6002	Peace	77
6003	Pastime	77
6004	Penalty	77
6005	Pendant	77
6006	People	77
6007	Perfect	77
6008	Period	77
6009	Perplex	77
6010	Pertain	77
6011	Parade	77
6012	Phantom	77
6013	Physical	77
6014	Pierce	77
6015	Piety	77
6016	Pillage	77
6017	Pillar	77
6018	Pure	77
6019	Pacha	76
6020	Packet	76
6023	Padlock	75
6024	Pagan	75
6025	Pageant	75
6026	Pagoda	75
6028	Painful	76
6029	Paynim	75
6032	Palace	76
6033	Palatine	76
6034	Palatable	76
6035	Palisade	76
6037	Palfrey	76
6038	Paste	75
6039	Puncheon	76
6040	Palladium	76
6041	Pallet	76
6042	Palm	76
6043	Palmetto	76
6044	Panacea	76
6045	Panoply	76
6046	Pantheist	77
6047	Pantomime	76
6049	Pannier	76
6050	Panama	76
6051	Pandour	76
6053	Panorama	75
6054	Paper	75
6056	Parachute	75
6057	Paraclete	75
6058	Paradise	76
6059	Paradox	76
6060	Parable	76
6061	Paragon	75
6062	Paragraph	76
6063	Parallel	76
6064	Paralyze	76
6065	Paramount	77
6072	Parasite	76
6073	Pardon	77
6075	Parental	75
6097	Pink	76
6098	Pinion	77
6099	Pine	77
6100	Pipe	76
6101	Radical	61
6103	Rainbow	61
6104	Ransom	61
6105	Rapture	58
6107	Rarely	60
6108	Ratable	61
6110	Rational	59
6111	Ravenous	59
6112	Readily	60
6114	Realism	46
6115	Realty	60
6116	Reaper	61
6117	Reasonable	60
6118	Receiver	66
6119	Recently	61
6128	Recital	60
6301	Safeguard	74
6302	Sagacity	74
6303	Sanitary	74
6304	Sampson	74
6305	Sanguine	74
6306	Sugar	74
6901	Piston	77
6902	Pitch	77

BRACKETS AND MODILLIONS

SCALE, 1½ Inches to 1 Foot.

No. 156.
Proj., 5½ in. Depth, 3½ in.
Face, 3 in.
Comp., $0.48 In parts, $0.30

No. 187.
Proj., 9¼ in. Depth, 6¼ in.
Face 5 in.
Comp., $0.90 In parts, $0.60

No. 42.
Proj., 7½ in. Depth, 4¼ in.
Face, 4¼ in.
Comp., $0.60 In parts, $0.30

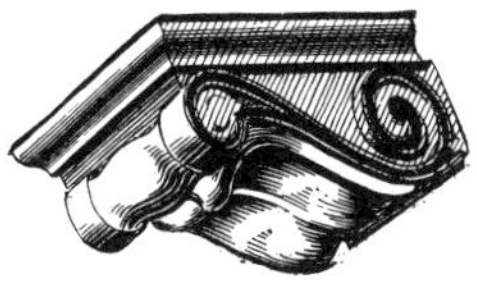

No. 153.
Proj., 11¼ in. Depth, 5 in.
Face, 5½ in.
Comp., $0.90 In parts, $0.60

No. 168.
Proj., 10 in. Depth, 4 in
Face, 2½ in.
Comp., $0.60 In parts, $0.40

No.	Projection.	Depth.	Face.	Complete.	In parts.
162	8 in.	5¼ in.	4 in.	$0.68	$0.45
225	10 "	6½ "	5 "	.90	.55
228	10 "	6½ "	6 "	1.00	.65
127	8 "	5½ "	5 "	.75	.50

No.	Projection.	Depth.	Face.	Complete.	In parts.
45	8½ in.	3½ in.	4¼ in.	$0.70	$0.40
46—Same size as No. 45, Roll front instead of Leaf				.60	.30

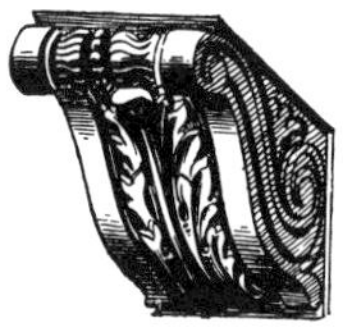

No.	Projection.	Depth.	Face.	Complete.	In parts.
47	6¼ in.	3½ in.	4¾ in.	$0.60	$0.30
WITH CAPS.					
47	6¾ in.	4¾ in.	4¾ in.	.70	.36

No. 199.
Proj., 14¾ in. Depth, 6 in.
Face, 7 in.
Comp., $1.50 In parts, $1.00

No. 198.
Proj., 12 in. Depth, 6¼ in.
Face, 7 in.
Comp., $1.20 In parts, $0.80

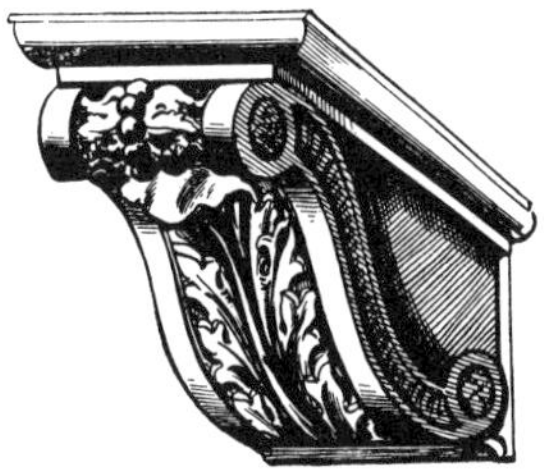

No. 55.
Proj., 10½ in. Depth, 7 in.
Face, 5½ in.
Comp., $1.00 In parts, $0.60

No. 234.
Proj., 7½ in. Depth, 4½ in.
Face, 5½ in.
Comp., $0.70 In parts, $0.45

No. 203.
Proj., 13 in. Depth, 10 in.
Face, 8 in.
Comp., $1.60 In parts, $1.05

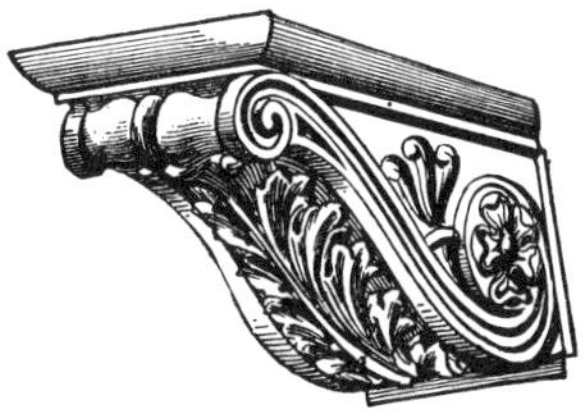

No.	Proj.	Depth.	Face.	Comp.	In parts.
224	9 in.	6 in.	4 in.	$0.72	$0.48
223	6½ "	4 "	3½ "	.55	.36

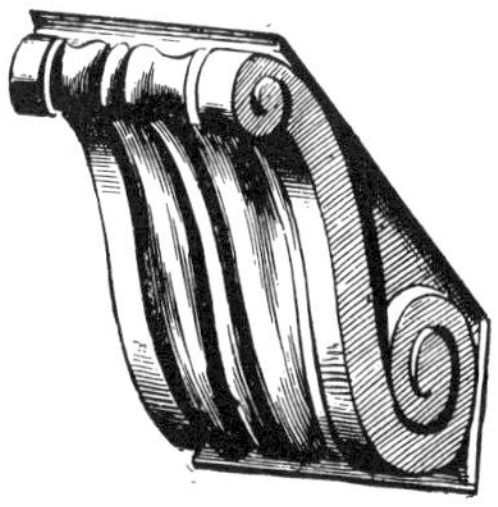

No.	Proj.	Depth.	Face.	Comp.	In parts.
122	10 in.	4 in.	6 in.	$0.70	$0.45
71	12½ "	5 "	5 "	1.10	.70

No.	Proj.	Depth.	Face.	Comp.	In parts.
177	12 in.	8 in.	6 in.	$1.40	$0.90
176	14½ "	8 "	6 "	1.65	1.10

No.	Proj.	Depth.	Face.	Comp.	In parts
20	13¼ in.	5¾ in.	6½ in.	$1.35	$0.85
28	11½ "	6 "	6 "	1.25	.75

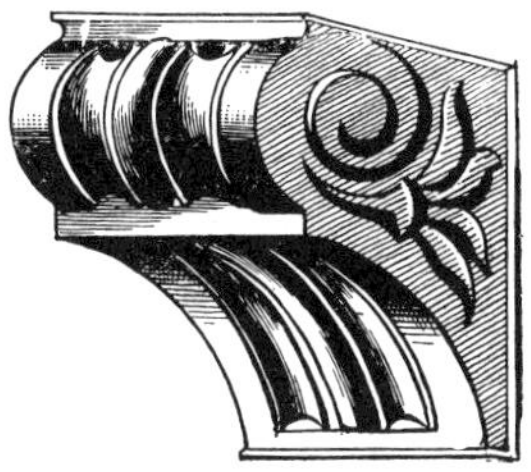

No.	Proj.	Depth.	Face.	Comp.	In parts.
38	6 in.	9½ in.	6 in.	$1.00	$0.55

No.	Proj.	Depth.	Face.	Comp.	In parts.
206	9 in.	14 in.	{7¾ in. 6⅜ "}	$1.90	$1.25

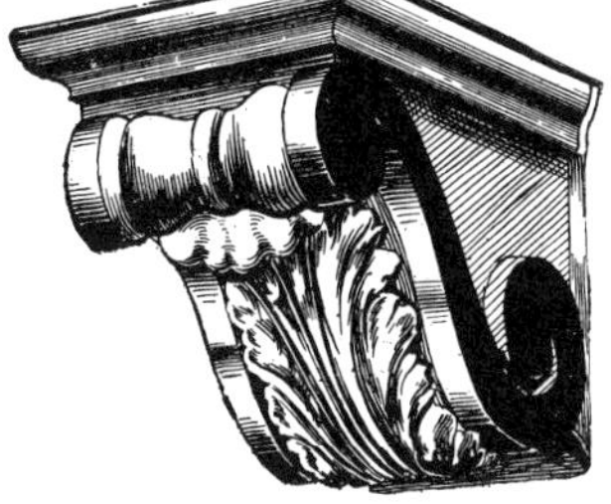

No.	Proj.	Depth.	Face.	Comp.	In parts.
164	13¼ in.	9 in.	8 in.	$2.10	$1.35

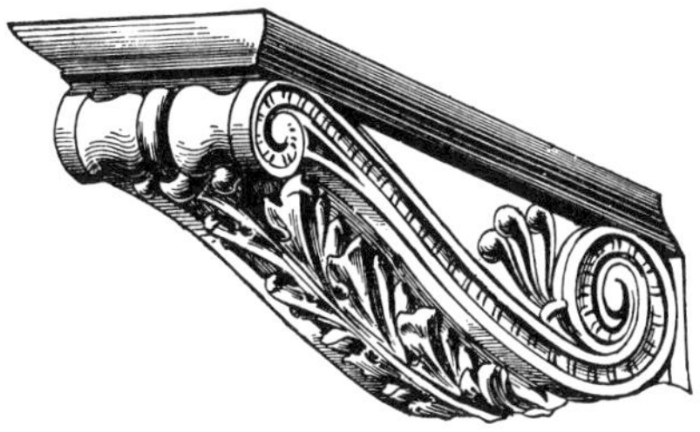

No.	Proj.	Depth.	Face.	Comp.	In parts.
233	14 in.	6 in.	5 in.	$1.20	$0.95

No.	Projection.	Depth.	Face.	Complete.	In parts.
131	12 in.	5 in.	6 in.	$1.00	$0.60
132	10 "	5 "	6 "	.95	.55
134	10 "	5 "	4 "	.85	.45
166	10 "	5 "	7 "	1.00	.60
165	12 "	5 "	7 "	1.10	.70
154	12 "	6 "	6 "	1.00	.65
77	12 "	6 "	7½ "	1.05	.70

No.	Projection.	Depth.	Face.	Complete.	In parts.
143	15 in.	7½ in.	8 in	$1.60	$1.00
144	15 "	7½ "	9 "	1.75	1.15
145	15 "	7½ "	7 "	1.50	.90
146	15 "	7½ "	6 "	1.45	.80
		ROLL FRONT.			
178	15 "	7½ in.	8 "	1.60	1.00
194	15 "	7½ "	10 "	1.70	1.20

No.	Projection.	Depth.	Face.	Complete.	In parts.
149	15 in.	9 in.	8 in.	$1.65	$1.05
147	15 "	9 "	6 "	1.50	.90
148	15 "	9 "	7 "	1.60	1.00
150	15 "	9 "	9 "	1.80	1.20
119	18¼ "	9¾ "	10 "	2.15	1.45
120	18¼ "	9¾ "	8 "	2.00	1.30
141	20½ "	9½ "	8 "	2.25	1.50
18	15¾ "	12 "	8 "	2.15	1.45
188	15 "	10 "	10 "	2.00	1.30
190	15 "	10 "	6 "	1.45	.95
191	15 "	10 "	7 "	1.55	1.05
192	15 "	10 "	8 "	1.65	1.10
193	15 "	10 "	9 "	1.80	1.20
7	18½ "	7½ "	9 "	2.00	1.30

No.	Projection.	Depth.	Face.	Complete.	In parts.
56	12½ in.	6½ in.	5½ in.	$1.35	$0.75

No.	Projection.	Depth.	Face.	Complete.	In parts.
230	14½ in.	7½ in.	6 in.	$1.35	$0.90

No.	Projection.	Depth.	Face.	Complete.	In parts.
37	9 in.	12¾ in.	6 in.	$1.15	$0.75
95	9 "	12¾ "	10 "	1.40	1.00

No. 95 has Roll Front without Leaf.

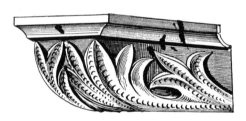

No.	Projection.	Depth.	Face.	Complete.	In parts.
216	15 in.	8 in.	6 in.	$1.65	$1.05

No.	Projection.	Depth.	Face.	Complete.	In parts.
229	13½ in.	9 in.	5 in.	$1.50	$1.00

No.	Projection.	Depth.	Face.	Complete.	In parts.
180	9½ in.	12 in.	{8½ in. / 4¾ "}	$1.40	$0.95

No.	Projection.	Depth.	Face.	Complete.	In parts.
226	13 in.	7 in.	6 in.	$1.20	$0.80

KEYSTONE.

No.	Projection.	Depth.	Face.	Complete.	In parts.
19	6 in.	13¼ in.	{8½ in / 5½ "}	$1.70	$1.20

No.	Projection.	Depth.	Face.	Complete.	In parts.
213	15 in.	9 in.	6 in.	$1.75	$1.15
269	15 "	9 "	7 "	1.80	1.20

No.	Projection.	Depth.	Face.	Complete.	In parts.
58	14½ in.	5½ in.	7 in.	$1.30	$0.75
121	18 "	7¼ "	7 "	1.70	1.15

No.	Projection.	Depth.	Face.	Complete.	In parts.
79	16 in.	10 in.	7½ in.	$2.25	$1.30
78	17 "	6 "	7½ "	2.00	1.15

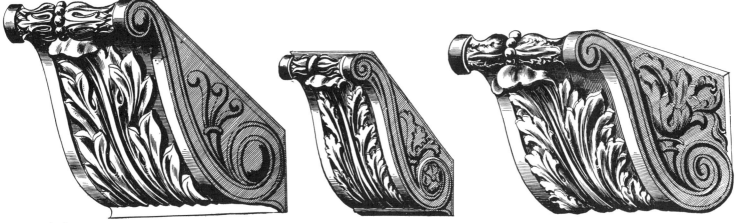

No.	Projection.	Depth.	Face.	Complete.	In parts.
11	20 in.	9 in.	12 in.	$2.75	$2.00

No.	Proj.	Depth.	Face.	Comp.	In parts.
126	15¾ in.	7 in.	7 in.	$1.40	$0.90

No.	Projection.	Depth.	Face.	Complete.	In parts.
3	17½ in.	16 in.	13 in.	$4.50	$3.00

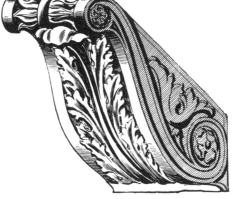

No.	Projection.	Depth.	Face.	Complete.	In parts.
123	19½ in.	7 in.	8 in.	$2.00	$1.30
124	18¼ "	8 "	8 "	1.90	1.20

No.	Projection.	Depth.	Face.	Complete.	In parts.
90	16½ in.	10 in.	10 in.	$2.15	$1.45

No.	Projection.	Depth.	Face.	Complete.	In parts.
183	19 in.	17 in.	10 in.	$3.75	$2.55

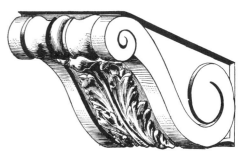

No.	Projection.	Depth.	Face.	Complete.	In parts.
235	17½ in.	8½ in.	10 in.	$2.10	$1.40

No.	Projection.	Depth.	Face.	Complete.	In parts.
70	12 in.	11½ in.	6 in.	$1.50	$1.00
142	14¾ "	24 "	6 "	2.60	1.90

No.	Projection.	Depth.	Face.	Complete.	In parts.
67	16 in.	8 in.	6½ in.	$1.65	$1.05

No.	Projection.	Depth.	Face.	Complete.	In parts.
135	12½ in.	8½ in.	11 in.	$1.80	$1.20

No.	Projection.	Depth.	Face.	Complete.	In parts.
140	17 in.	8¼ in.	10½ in.	$2.00	$1.35

No.	Projection.	Depth.	Face.	Complete.	In parts.
186	18 in.	13 in.	10 in.	$2.75	$1.95

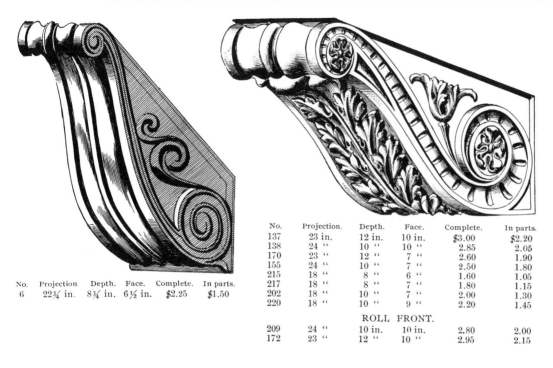

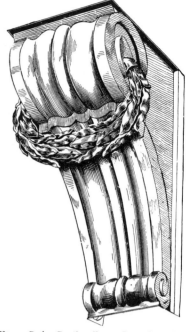

No.	Projection.	Depth.	Face.	Complete.	In parts.
137	23 in.	12 in.	10 in.	$3.00	$2.20
138	24 "	10 "	10 "	2.85	2.05
170	23 "	12 "	7 "	2.60	1.90
155	24 "	10 "	7 "	2.50	1.80
215	18 "	8 "	6 "	1.60	1.05
217	18 "	8 "	7 "	1.80	1.15
202	18 "	10 "	7 "	2.00	1.30
220	18 "	10 "	9 "	2.20	1.45

ROLL FRONT.

209	24 "	10 in.	10 in.	2.80	2.00
172	23 "	12 "	10 "	2.95	2.15

No.	Projection	Depth.	Face.	Complete.	In parts.
6	22¾ in.	8¾ in.	6½ in.	$2.25	$1.50

No.	Proj.	Depth.	Face.	Comp.	In parts.
212	15 in.	24 in.	{ 10 in. / 7 " }	$4.00	$2.70

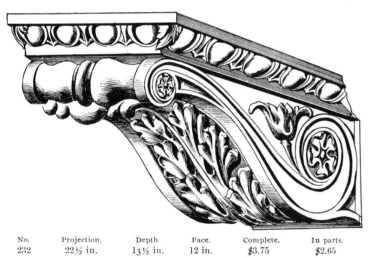

No.	Projection.	Depth.	Face.	Complete.	In parts.
232	22½ in.	13½ in.	12 in.	$3.75	$2.65

No.	Projection	Depth.	Face.	Complete.	In parts.
104	18½ in.	8½ in.	9½ in.	$2.50	$1.50

FOOT LEAVES

SCALE, 1½ Inches to 1 Foot

No.	Size.	Each.
908	6 x 3¾ in.	$0.12

No.	Size.	Each.
907	6½ x 7 in.	$0.27

No.	Size.	Each.
906	6¼ x 9¼ in.	$0.38

No.	Size.	Each.
910	6 x 4½ in.	$0.18

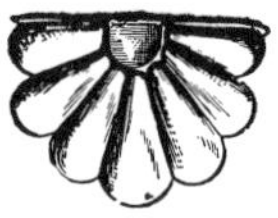

No.	Size.	Each.
911	4¼ x 6 in.	$0.12

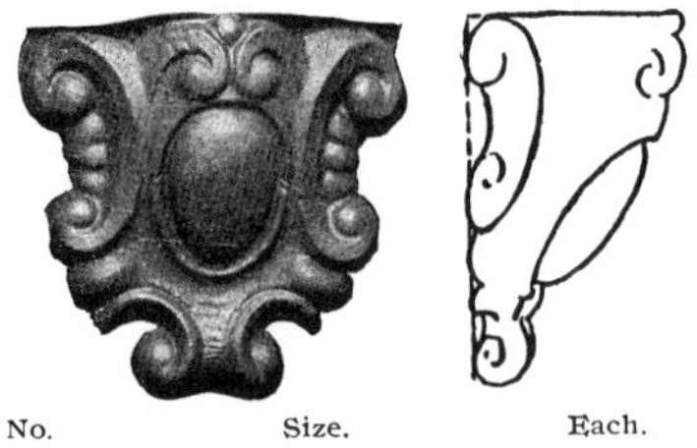

No.	Size.	Each.
912	8½ x 8½ x 3¼ in.	$0.30

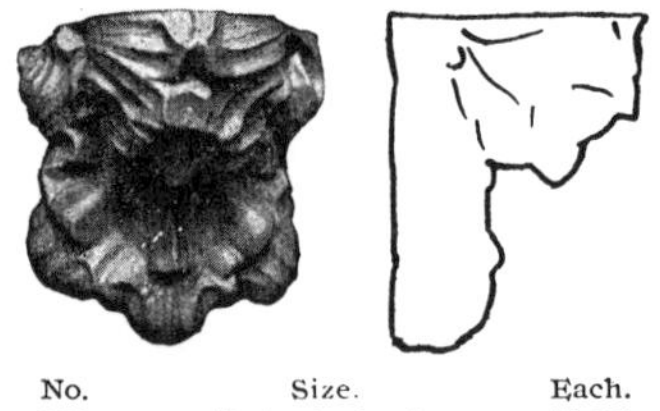

No.	Size.	Each.
922	7½ x 7½ x 6	$0.36

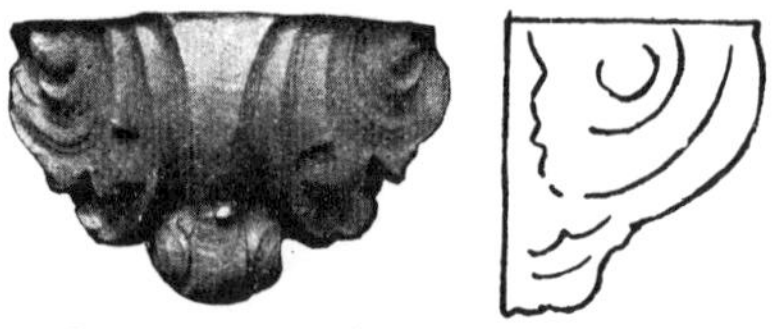

No.	Size.	In parts.
920	6 x 10 x 5½ in.	$0.33

No.	Size.	Each.
926	8¾ x 6½ x 1½	$0.21

No	Size.	Each.
927	5½ x 8 x 1½ in	$0.18

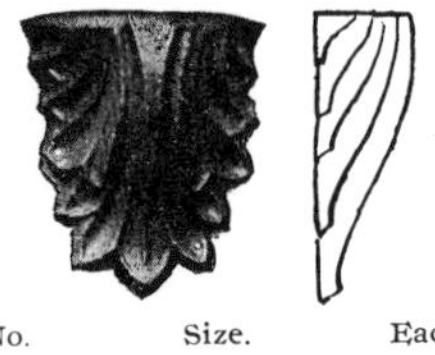

No.	Size.	Each.
925	6½ x 5½ x 2½ in.	$0.22

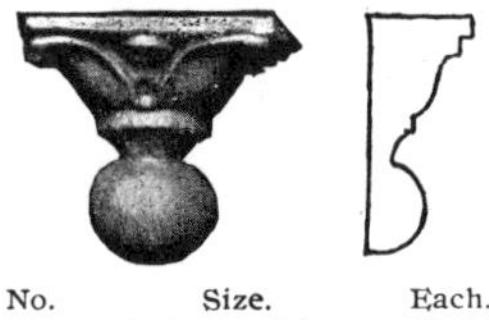

No.	Size.	Each.
914	5½ x 6 x 2 in.	$0.23

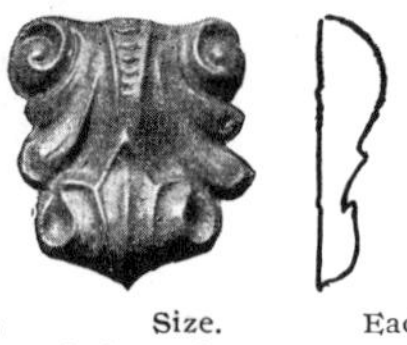

No.	Size.	Each.
913	6¼ x 5½ x 1½	$0.18

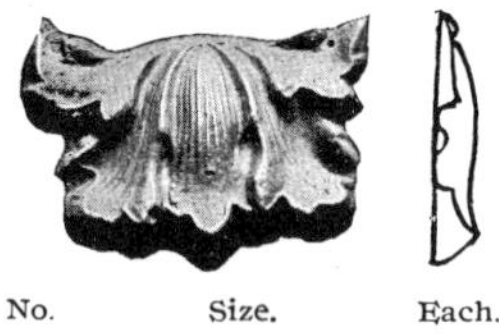

No.	Size.	Each.
928	5¾ x 8½ x 1½	$0.18

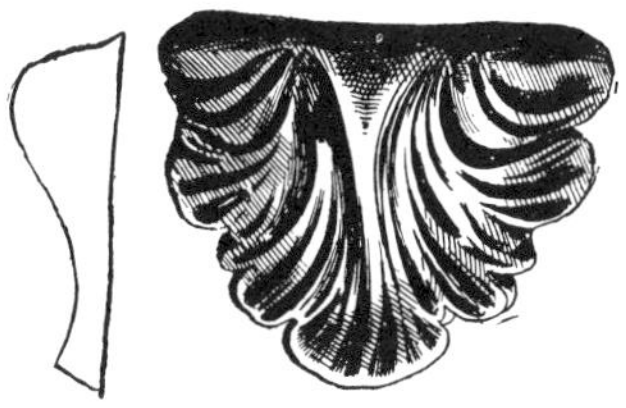

No. 902 Size. 8¾ x 11½ in. Each. $0.33

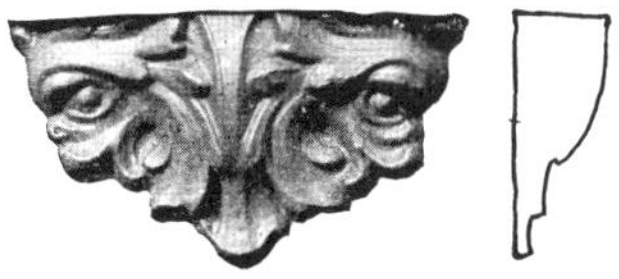

No. 916 Size. 6 x 11 x 2½ Each. $0.24

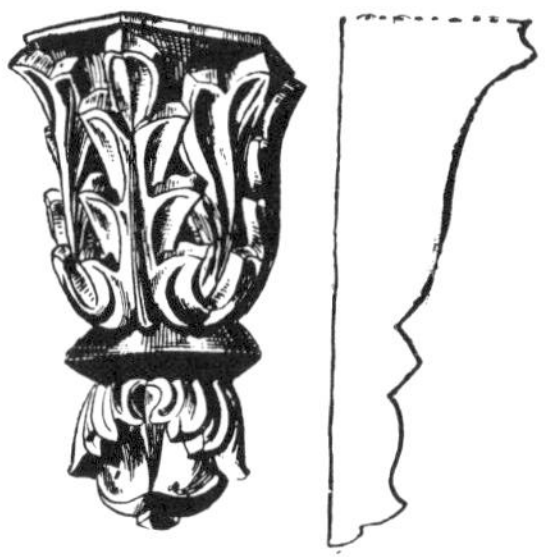

No. 904 Size. 12x6 in. Complete. $0.60 In parts. $0.40

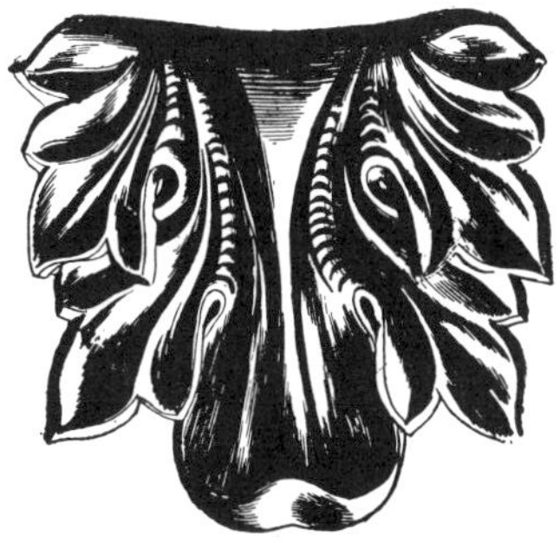

No. 901 Size. 14½ x 13 in. Each. $0.75

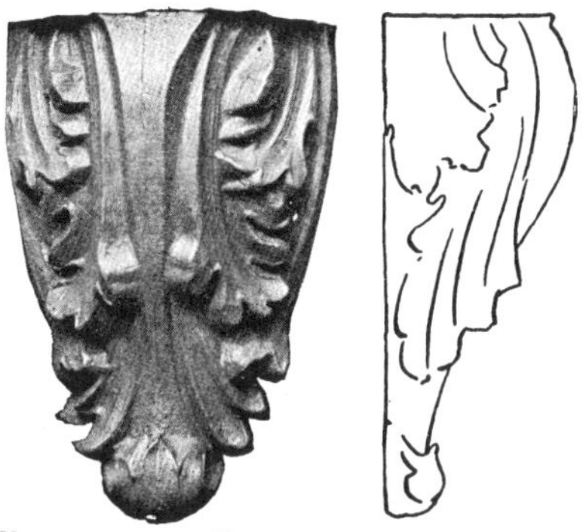

No. 921 Size. 16 x 10 x 5 in. In parts. $0.66

BRACKET FRONTS AND LEAVES

SCALE, 1½ inches to 1 foot

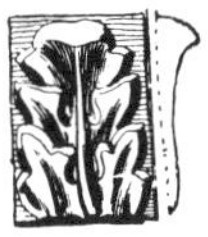

No. 427 Size. 3½ x 5 in. Each. $0.08

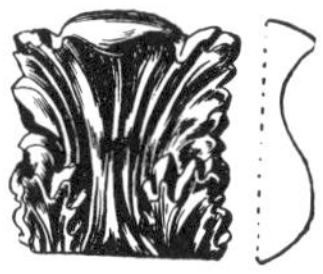

No. 438 Size. 5½ x 6 in. Each. $0.14

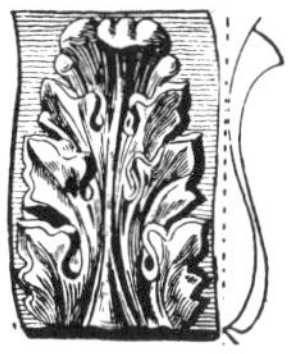

No. 424 Size. 5 x 7¼ in. Each. $0.12

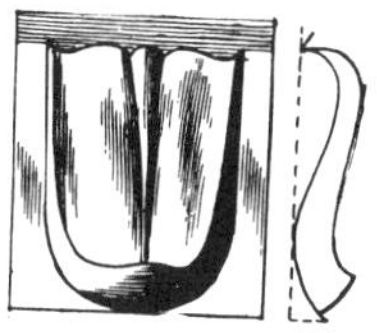

No. 329 Size. 6 x 7 Each. $0.18

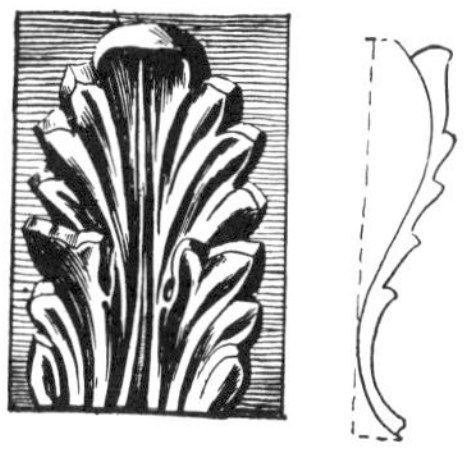

No. 303 Size. 6 x 9½ Each. $0.20

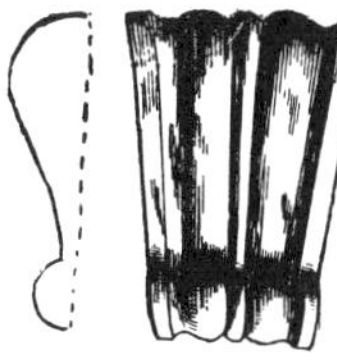

No.	Size.	Each.
367	3¾x5½x8½in.	$0.30
368	9 x 11½x13 "	0.60

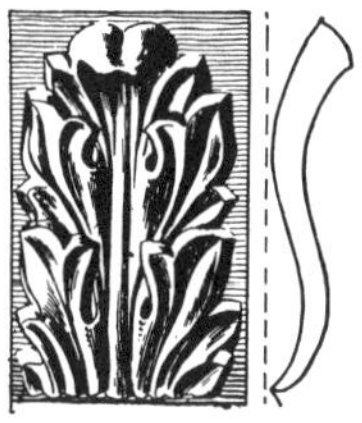

No. 331 Size. 6 x 9 in. Each. $0.20

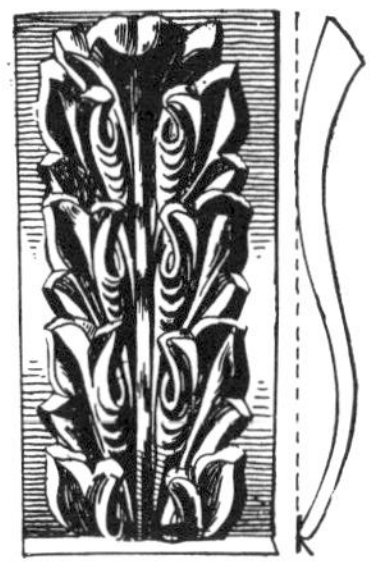

No.	Size.	Each.
352	6 x 12 in.	$0.24
326	6 x 13 "	0.27

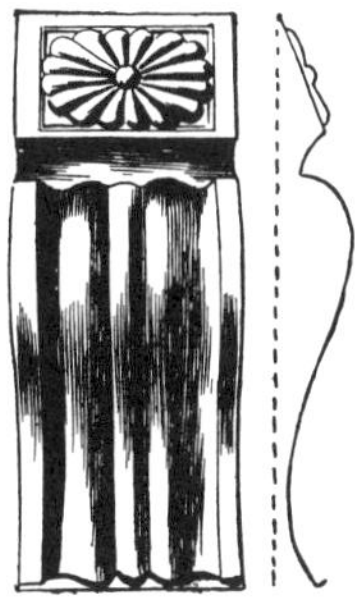

No.	Size.	Each.
451	5¾ x 15¾ in.	$0.30
387	5½ x 18 "	0.34
452	5½ x 13 "	0.24

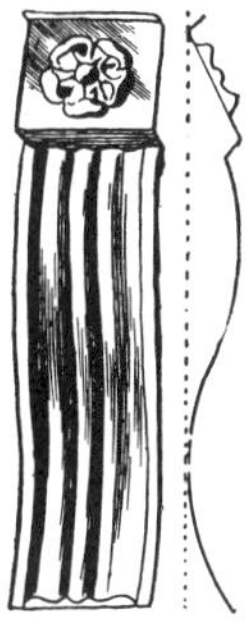

No. 386 Size. 3½ x 14 in. Each. $0.18

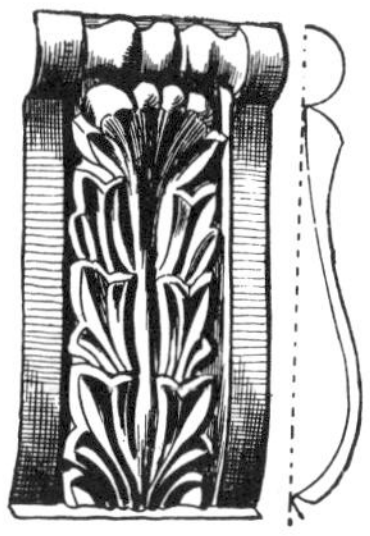

No. 305 Size. 6¼ x 12 in. Each. $0.24

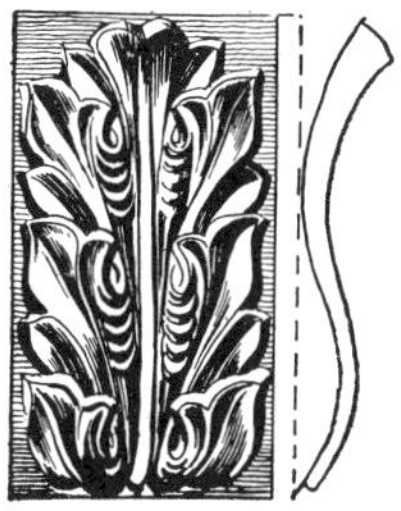

No. 301 Size. 6 x 11½ in. Each. $0.21

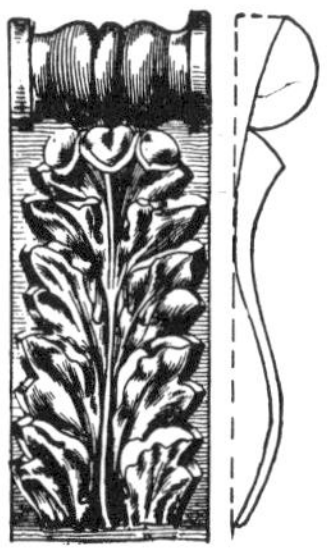

No. 304 Size. 5 x 12 in. Each. $0.21

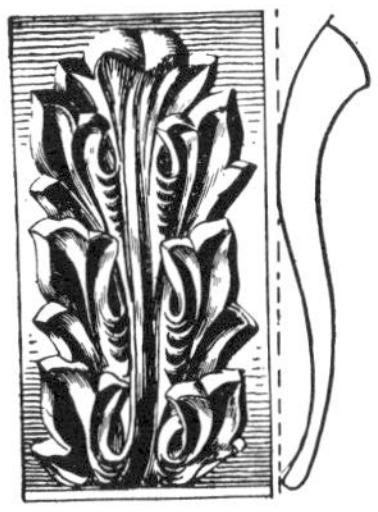

No. 302 Size. 6 x 10½ in. Each. $0.20

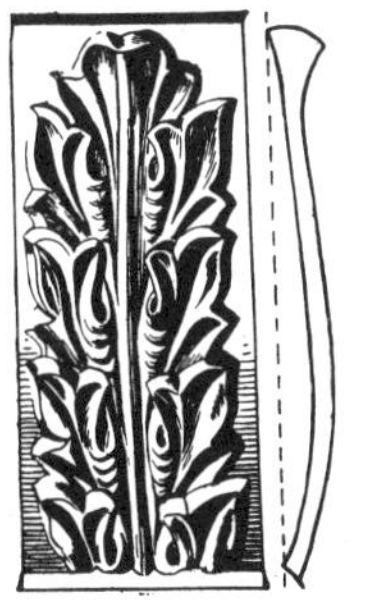

No. 328 Size. 6 x 13 in. Each. $0.27

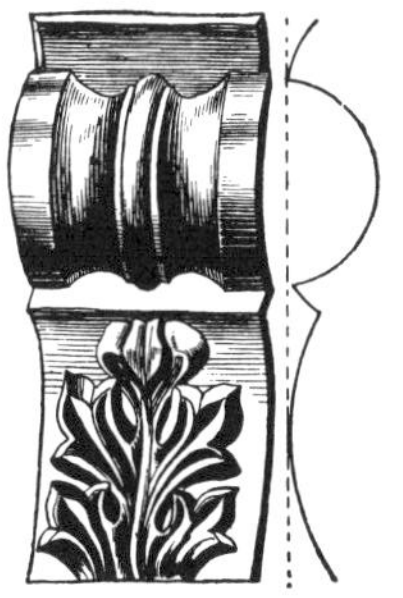

No. 309 Size. 6 x 13¼ in. Each. $0.27

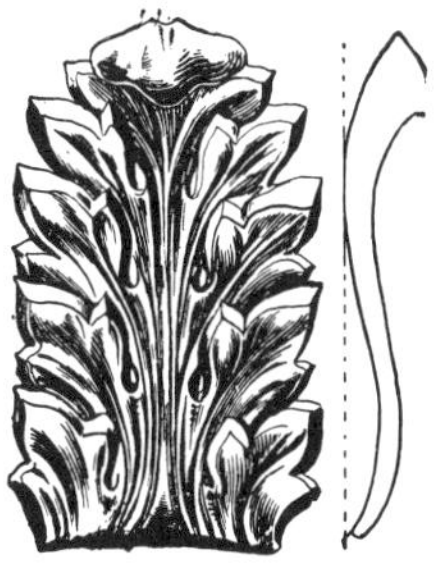

No.	Size.	Each.
431	8 x 12 in.	$0.30
432	8 x 10 "	0.24

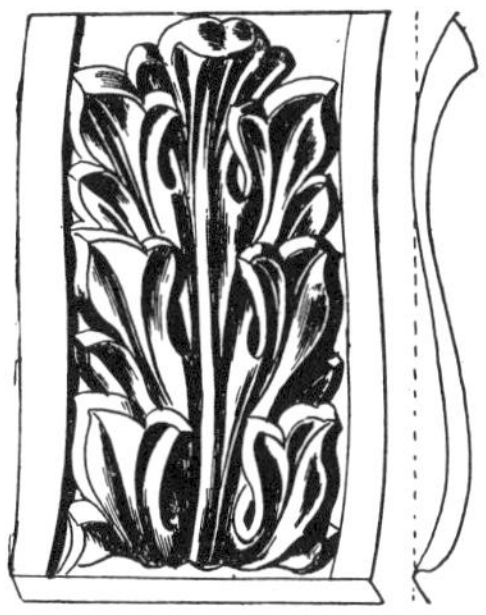

No. 319 Size. 9 x 13¼ in. Each $0.38

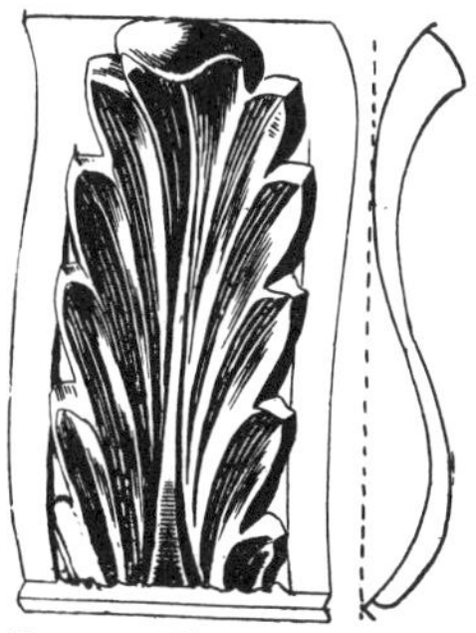

No. 312 Size. 8 x 13½ in. Each. $0.30

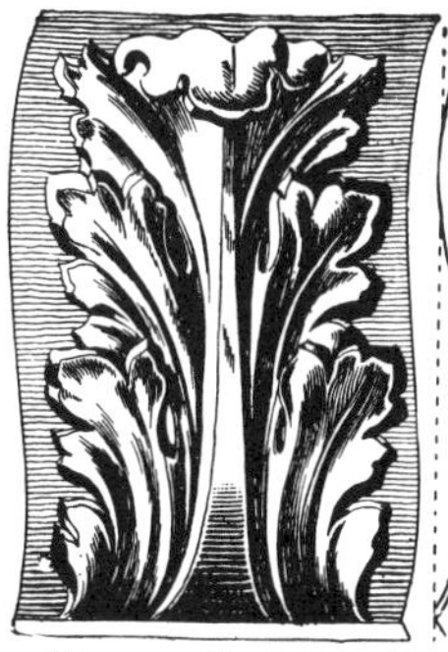

No. 320 Size. 10 x 14½ in Each. $0.45

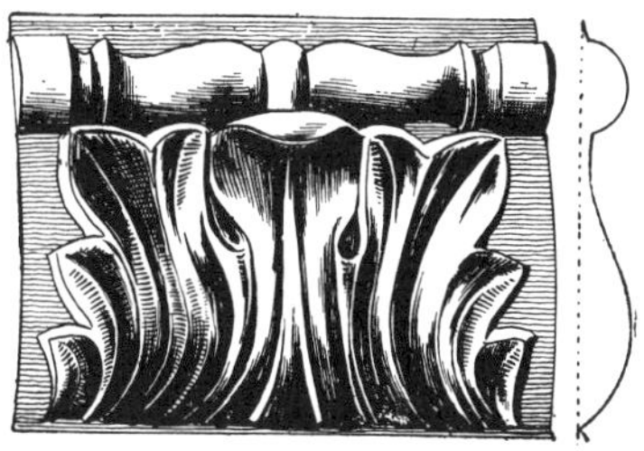

No.	Size.	Each.
334	15 x 11 in.	$0.50
332	12 x 7½ "	.30

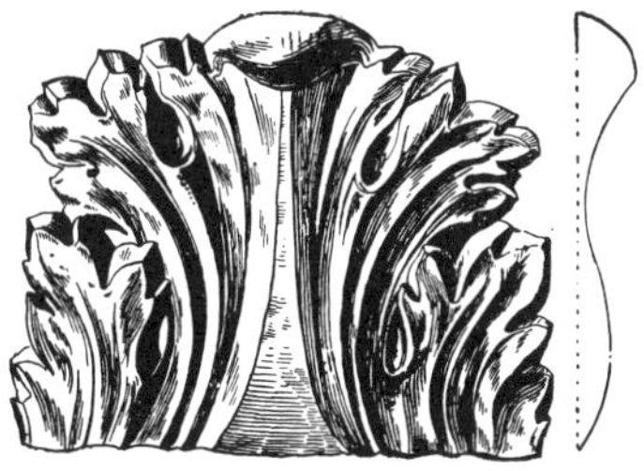

No. 437 Size. 11½ x 15 in. Each $0.38

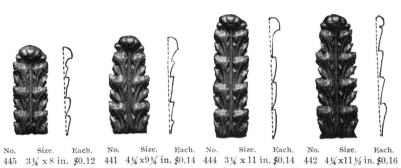

   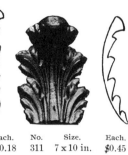  

No.	Size.	Each.	No.	Size.	Each.	No.	Size.	Each.	No.	Size.	Each.	No.	Size.	Each.	No.	Size.	Each.
445	3¼ x 8 in.	$0.12	441	4¼ x 9¼ in.	$0.14	444	3¼ x 11 in.	$0.14	442	4¼ x 11½ in.	$0.16	443	5¼ x 11 in.	$0.18	311	7 x 10 in.	$0.45

No.	Size.	Each.
463	6 x 13 in.	$0.25

 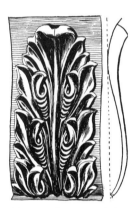 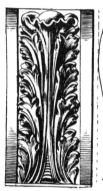 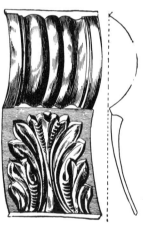  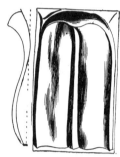

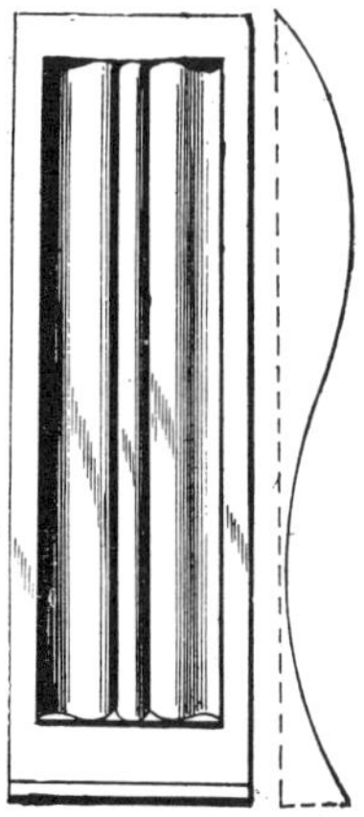

No.	Size.	Each.	No.	Size.	Each.	No.	Size.	Each.	No.	Size.	Each.
325	6 x 19½ in.	$0.33	338	9 x 17½ in.	$0.45	350	7 x 16½ in.	$0.38	390	8 x 16½ in.	$0.38

No.	Size.	Each.
316	8 x 12½ in.	$0.36
317	8 x 14½ "	.41
389	5 x 9 "	.15

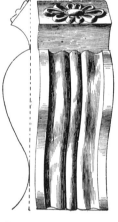 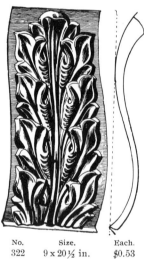 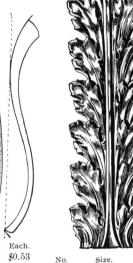

No.	Size.	Each.	No.	Size.	Each.	No.	Size.	Each.	No.	Size.	Each.
439	7½ x 20 in.	$0.44	384	7 x 20 in.	$0.42	310	9 x 21 in.	$0.60	322	9 x 20½ in.	$0.53

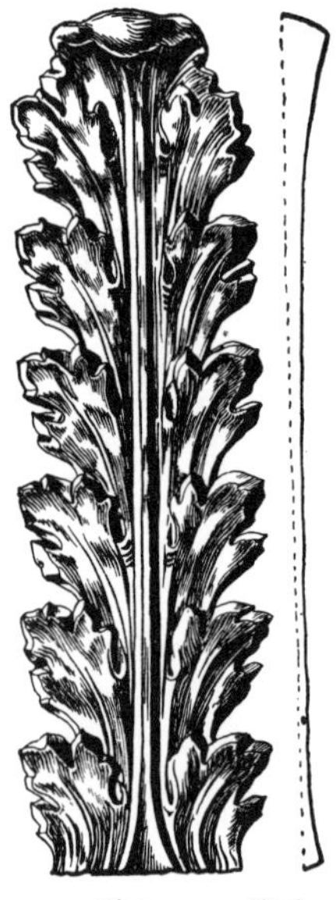

No.	Size.	Each.
379	4 x 26 in.	$0.36
380	6 x 25 "	.45
381	8 x 26 "	.55
382	10 x 25 "	.65
383	12 x 27 "	.90

These can be made any length.

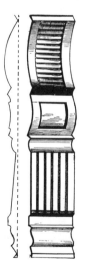   

No.	Size.	Per ft.
5502	6 in.	$0.19
5510	2 "	.07½
5511	2½ "	.09
5507	3 "	.10½
5512	3½ "	.12
5508	4 "	.13½
5513	4½ "	.15
5509	5 "	.16½
5501	8 "	.27
5514	6½ "	.23

Can be bent any shape or curve.

No.	Size.	Width.	Price.
513	4 in.	10 in.	$0.18
514	4½ "	10 "	.21
515	5 "	10 "	.24
516	5½ "	10 "	.27
517	6 "	10 "	.30
518	4 "	12 "	.21
519	4½ "	12 "	.24
520	5 "	12 "	.27
521	5½ "	12 "	.30
522	6 "	12 "	.33

No.	Diam.	Width	Price.
506	3 in.	7 in.	$0.11
507	3½ "	7 "	.13
508	4 "	7 "	.15
509	4½ "	7 "	.17
510	3½ "	9 "	.12
511	4½ "	9 "	.18
512	5 "	9 "	.21

No.	Diam.	Width.	Price.
523	2½ in.	6 in.	$0.08
524	3 "	6 "	.10
525	3½ "	6 "	.12
526	4 "	6 "	.14
527	3 "	8 "	.12
528	3½ "	8 "	.14
529	4 "	8 "	.16
530	4½ "	8 "	.18
531	5 "	8 "	.21
501	4 "	9 "	.15

No.	Size.	Each.
324	4 x 21 in.	$0.30

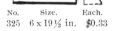

307.

6 x 13½ in.   Each, $0.25

335.

No.	Size.	Each.
335	8 x 17 in.	$0.51
336	9 x 17 "	0.54
337	7 x 17 "	0.45
339	6 x 17 "	0.40
340	10 x 17 "	0.60

453

4 x 16 in.   Each, $0.24

321.

No.	Size.	Each.
321	7 x 18 in.	$0.45
315	8 x 18 "	.51
318	6 x 18 "	.40
330	9 x 18 "	.54
345	10 x 18 "	.60

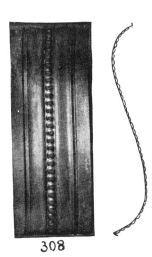

308

7½ x 20 in.   Each, $0.45

393.

10 x 18 in.   Each, $0.51

448

13½ x 19 in.   Each, $0.90

394

8 x 26 in.   In parts, $0.75

450.

7 x 26½ in.   Each, $0.60

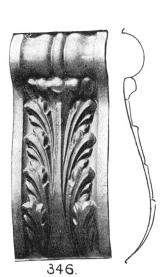

346.

9 x 21 in.   Each, $0.60

341

10 x 23½ in.   Each, $0.72

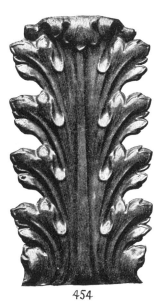

454

14 x 25 in.   Each, $1.00

391

12 x 23 in.   Each, $0.90

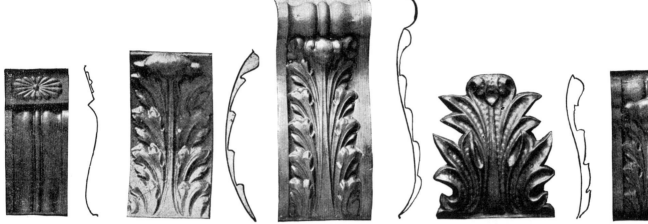

No. 440 6 x 13 in. Each, $0.25 No. 392 8 x 15 in. Each, $0.42 No. 343 9 x 21 in. Each, $0.60 No. 464 12 x 13 in. Each, $0.45 No. 342 7½ x 14 in. Each, $0.36

PANEL ENRICHMENTS

SCALE, 1½ Inches to 1 Foot

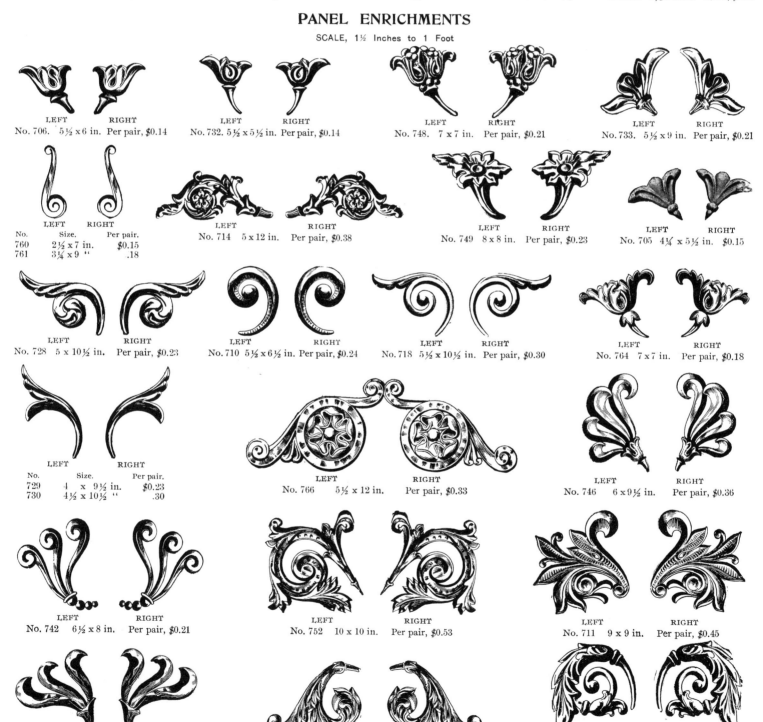

LEFT   RIGHT
No. 706. 5½ x 6 in. Per pair, $0.14

LEFT   RIGHT
No. 732. 5½ x 5½ in. Per pair, $0.14

LEFT   RIGHT
No. 748. 7 x 7 in. Per pair, $0.21

LEFT   RIGHT
No. 733. 5½ x 9 in. Per pair, $0.21

No.	Size.	Per pair.
760	2½ x 7 in.	$0.15
761	3¼ x 9 "	.18

LEFT   RIGHT
No. 714 5 x 12 in. Per pair, $0.38

LEFT   RIGHT
No. 749 8 x 8 in. Per pair, $0.23

LEFT   RIGHT
No. 705 4¼ x 5½ in. $0.15

LEFT   RIGHT
No. 728 5 x 10½ in. Per pair, $0.23

LEFT   RIGHT
No. 710 5½ x 6½ in. Per pair, $0.24

LEFT   RIGHT
No. 718 5½ x 10½ in. Per pair, $0.30

LEFT   RIGHT
No. 764 7 x 7 in. Per pair, $0.18

No.	Size.	Per pair.
729	4 x 9½ in.	$0.23
730	4½ x 10½ "	.30

LEFT   RIGHT
No. 766 5½ x 12 in. Per pair, $0.33

LEFT   RIGHT
No. 746 6 x 9½ in. Per pair, $0.36

LEFT   RIGHT
No. 742 6½ x 8 in. Per pair, $0.21

LEFT   RIGHT
No. 752 10 x 10 in. Per pair, $0.53

LEFT   RIGHT
No. 711 9 x 9 in. Per pair, $0.45

LEFT   RIGHT
No. 713 9 x 9 in. Per pair, $0.33

LEFT   RIGHT
No. 757 11½ x 6 in. Per pair, $0.33

LEFT   RIGHT
No. 753 7½ x 9 in. Per pair, $0.42

LEFT   RIGHT   LEFT   RIGHT

No.   Per pair.   No.   Per pair.
739   3 x 9 in. $0.18   727   4½ x 9 in. $0.21

LEFT   RIGHT

No. 765   6 x 12½ in.   Per pair, $0.35

LEFT   RIGHT

No. 712   6½ x 14 in.   Per pair, $0.53

LEFT   RIGHT

No. 754   10½ x 11½ in.   Per pair, $0.57

LEFT   RIGHT

No. 701   9 x 18 in.   Per pair, $0.60

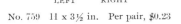

LEFT   RIGHT   LEFT   RIGHT   LEFT   RIGHT   LEFT   RIGHT

No. 759   11 x 3½ in.   Per pair, $0.23   No. 703   9 x 18 in.   Per pair, $0.72   No. 725   5½ x 14 in.   Per pair, $0.38   No. 771   5 x 13 in.   Per pair, $0.36

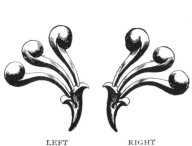

LEFT   RIGHT   LEFT   RIGHT   LEFT   RIGHT

No. 740   9 x 9½ in.   Per pair, $0.30   No. 707   13 x 13 in.   Per pair, $0.66   No. 774   9 x 13¾ in.   Per pair, $0.66

LEFT   RIGHT   LEFT   RIGHT   LEFT   RIGHT   LEFT   RIGHT

No. 734   5 x 13 in.   Per pair, $0.33   No. 755   5½ x 11½ in.   Per pair, $0.30   No. 735   4 x 7¾ in.   Per pair, $0.23   No. 769   5x9 in.   Per pair, $0.30

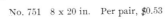

LEFT   RIGHT   LEFT   RIGHT

No. 751   8 x 20 in.   Per pair, $0.53   No. 741   6 x 16 in.   Per pair, $0.55

BROSCHART & BRAUN : NEW YORK.

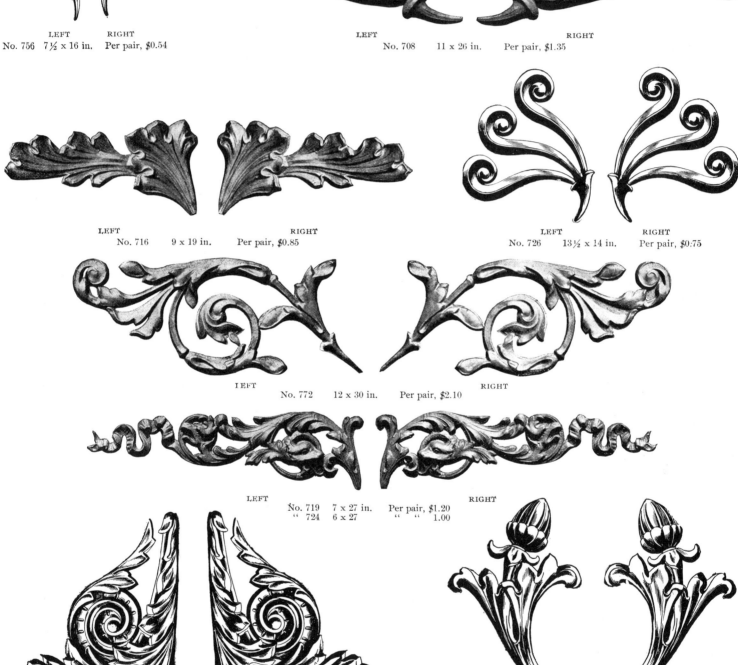

LEFT   RIGHT

No. 756   7½ x 16 in.   Per pair, $0.54

LEFT   RIGHT

No. 708   11 x 26 in.   Per pair, $1.35

LEFT   RIGHT

No. 716   9 x 19 in.   Per pair, $0.85

LEFT   RIGHT

No. 726   13½ x 14 in.   Per pair, $0.75

LEFT   RIGHT

No. 772   12 x 30 in.   Per pair, $2.10

LEFT   RIGHT

No. 719   7 x 27 in.   Per pair, $1.20
"   724   6 x 27   "   "   1.00

LEFT   RIGHT

No. 723   19 x 19 in.   Per pair, $1.28

LEFT   RIGHT

No. 762   13½ x 19 in.   Per pair, $0.90

LEFT   RIGHT

No. 717   7 x 27 in.   Per pair, $1.20
"   731   6 x 27   "   "   1.00

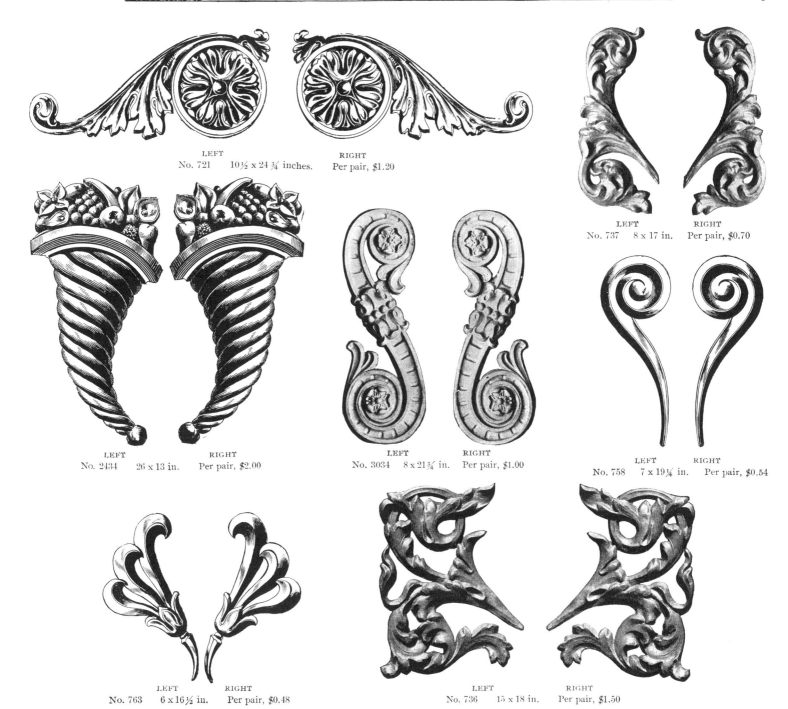

LEFT   RIGHT
No. 721   10½ x 24 ¾ inches.   Per pair, $1.20

LEFT   RIGHT
No. 737   8 x 17 in.   Per pair, $0.70

LEFT   RIGHT
No. 2434   26 x 13 in.   Per pair, $2.00

LEFT   RIGHT
No. 3034   8 x 21¾ in.   Per pair, $1.00

LEFT   RIGHT
No. 758   7 x 19¼ in.   Per pair, $0.54

LEFT   RIGHT
No. 763   6 x 16½ in.   Per pair, $0.48

LEFT   RIGHT
No. 736   15 x 18 in.   Per pair, $1.50

EGG AND DART ENRICHMENTS

SCALE, 1½ Inches to 1 Foot

No. 1121   1⅛ inches, exclusive of Flanges . . . . Per foot, $0.05

No 1116   2½ inches, exclusive of Flanges . . . . Per foot, .11
" 1112   4¼ "   "   "   "   .16

No. 1114   2½ inches, exclusive of Flanges . . . . Per foot, .09

No. 1135   4 inches, exclusive of Flanges . . . . Per foot, .16

No. 1146   1 inch . . . . Per foot, $0.06

No. 1155   1¼ inches . . . . Per foot, .07

No. 1160   1¼ inches . . . . Per foot, .07

No. 1144   1½ inches . . . . Per foot, .07

No. 1152   2½ inches . . . . Per foot, .10

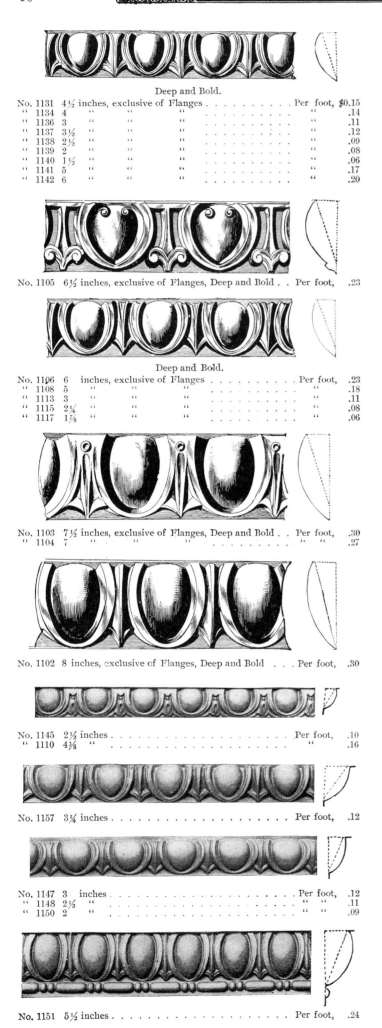

Deep and Bold.

No. 1131	4½ inches, exclusive of Flanges	. . . . Per foot,	$0.15
" 1134	4 " " "	. . . . "	.14
" 1136	3 " " "	. . . . "	.11
" 1137	3½ " " "	. . . . "	.12
" 1138	2½ " " "	. . . . "	.09
" 1139	2 " " "	. . . . "	.08
" 1140	1½ " " "	. . . . "	.06
" 1141	5 " " "	. . . . "	.17
" 1142	6 " " "	. . . . "	.20

No. 1105   6½ inches, exclusive of Flanges, Deep and Bold . . Per foot,   .23

Deep and Bold.

No. 1106	6 inches, exclusive of Flanges	. . . . Per foot,	.23
" 1108	5 " " "	. . . . "	.18
" 1113	3 " " "	. . . . "	.11
" 1115	2¼ " " "	. . . . "	.08
" 1117	1⅞ " " "	. . . . "	.06

No. 1103   7½ inches, exclusive of Flanges, Deep and Bold . . Per foot,   .30
" 1104   7   "   "   " . . . . "   .27

No. 1102   8 inches, exclusive of Flanges, Deep and Bold . . . Per foot,   .30

No. 1145   2½ inches . . . . Per foot,   .10
" 1110   4⅜ " . . . . "   .16

No. 1157   3¼ inches . . . . Per foot,   .12

No. 1147   3 inches . . . . Per foot,   .12
" 1148   2½ " . . . . "   .11
" 1150   2 " . . . . "   .09

No. 1151   5½ inches . . . . Per foot,   .24

No. 1143   3⅜ inches . . . . Per foot, $0.12

No. 1159   3½ inches . . . . Per foot,   .13

No. 1165   4 inches . . . . Per foot,   .15

No. 1163   6 inches . . . . Per foot,   .27

No. 1164   6 inches . . . . Per foot,   .27

No. 1149   6 inches . . . . Per foot,   .27

No. 1154   7½ inches . . . . Per foot,   .32

No. 1161   7 inches . . . . Per foot,   .33
" 1166   5 " . . . . "   .22

No. 1162   7 inches . . . . Per foot,   .33

No. 1158   7½ inches . . . . Per foot,   .36

OGEE ENRICHMENTS

SCALE, 1½ Inches to 1 Foot

No. 1417 1⅛ inches, exclusive of Flanges . . . . Per foot, $0.05
" 1418 ⅞ " " " . . . . " .05
" 1419 ⅝ " " " . . . . " .05

No. 1414 1¾ inches, exclusive of Flanges . . . . Per foot, .08

No. 1449 3 inches, exclusive of Flanges . . . . Per foot, .11
" 1450 3½ " " " . . . . " .12
" 1451 4 " " " . . . . " .14
" 1452 5 " " " . . . . " .17
" 1402 5½ " " " . . . . " .20
" 1404 4¼ " " " . . . . " .14
" 1416 1⅜ " " " . . . . " .06

No. 1447 3 inches, exclusive of Flanges . . . . Per foot, .12
" 1448 4 " " " . . . . " .14

No. 1453 3¾ inches . . . . Per foot, .14

No. 1435 4 inches . . . . Per foot, .14

No. 1456 4 inches, exclusive of Flanges . . . . Per foot, .13½
" 1446 2¾ " " " . . . . " .09
" 1460 1½ " " " . . . . " .07

No. 1457 5 inches, exclusive of Flanges . . . . Per foot, .15

No. 1433 5½ inches . . . . Per foot, .20

No. 1431 6 inches . . . . Per foot, .21

No. 1401 5¾ inches, exclusive of Flanges . . . . Per foot, .21

No. 1415 1⅜ inches, exclusive of Flanges . . . . Per foot, .06

No. 1409 2⅜ inches, exclusive of Flanges . . . . Per foot, .09
" 1408 3½ " " " . . . . " .15

No. 1412 2⅝ inches, exclusive of Flanges . . . . Per foot, .12
" 1413 1¾ " without Beading . . . . " .08

No. 1410 3¼ inches, exclusive of Flanges . . . . Per foot, .12
" 1411 2¼ " without Beading . . . . " .08

No. 1406 3¼ inches, exclusive of Flanges . . . . Per foot, .12

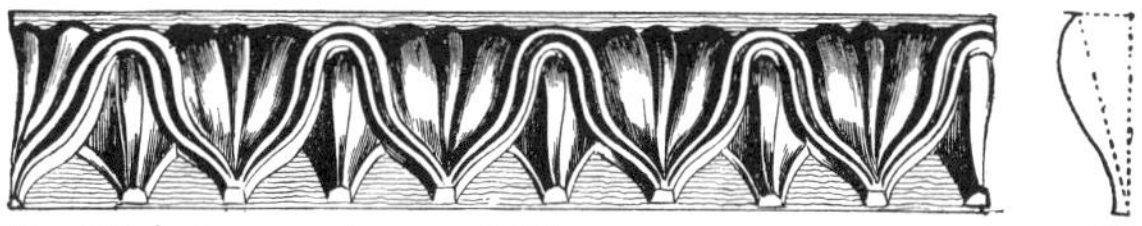

No. 1405 4¼ inches, exclusive of Flanges . . . . Per foot, .14

No. 1454 3½ inches . . . . Per foot, .14

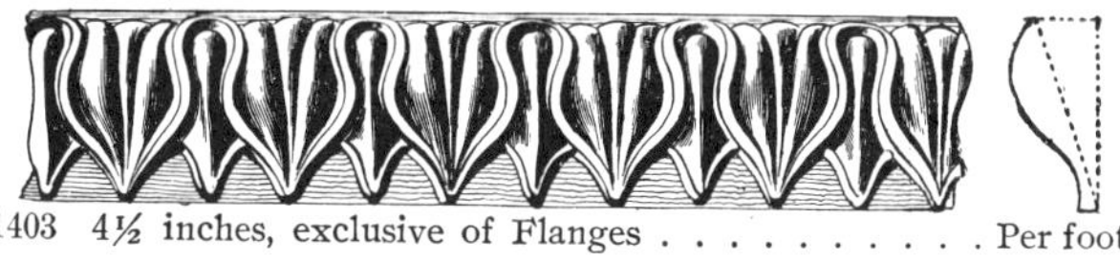

No. 1403 4½ inches, exclusive of Flanges . . . . Per foot, .18

No. 1432 6 inches . . . . Per foot, .21

No. 1427 7¾ inches . . . . Per foot, .33

No. 1424 14¼ inches . . . . Per foot, .48

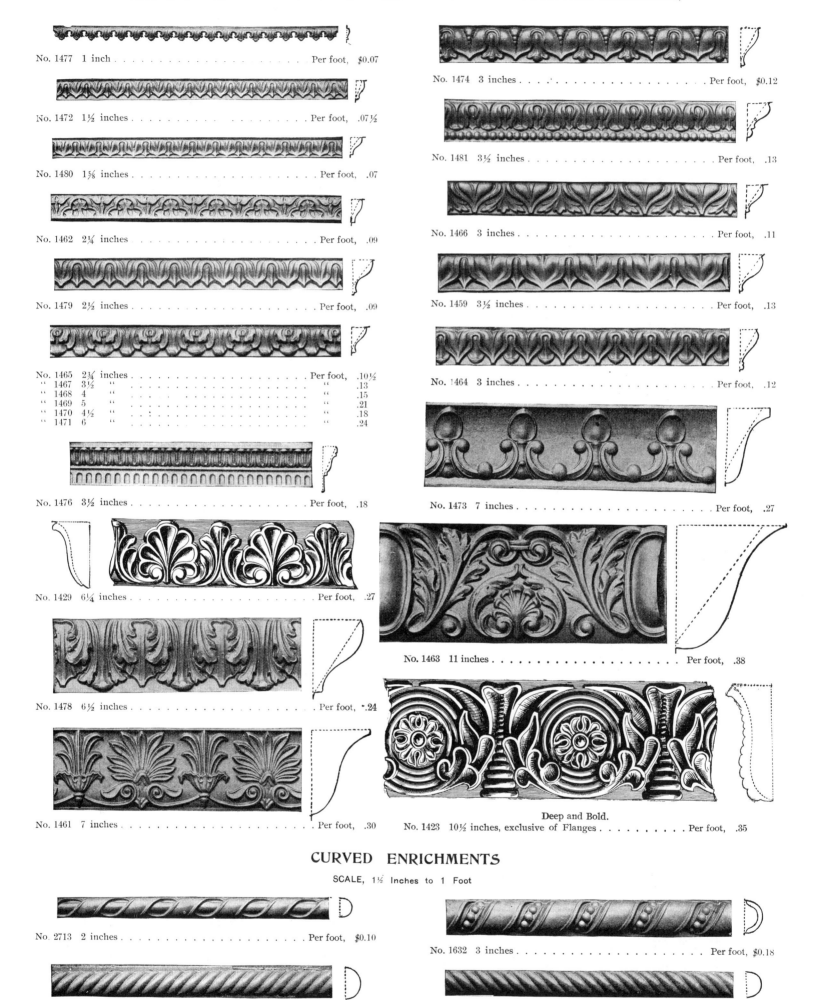

No. 1477   1 inch . . . . Per foot, $0.07

No. 1472   1½ inches . . . . Per foot, .07½

No. 1480   1⅝ inches . . . . Per foot, .07

No. 1462   2¼ inches . . . . Per foot, .09

No. 1479   2½ inches . . . . Per foot, .09

No. 1465   2¾ inches . . . . Per foot, .10½
"   1467   3½   "   .13
"   1468   4   "   .15
"   1469   5   "   .21
"   1470   4½   "   .18
"   1471   6   "   .24

No. 1476   3½ inches . . . . Per foot, .18

No. 1429   6¼ inches . . . . Per foot, .27

No. 1478   6½ inches . . . . Per foot, .24

No. 1461   7 inches . . . . Per foot, .30

No. 1474   3 inches . . . . Per foot, $0.12

No. 1481   3½ inches . . . . Per foot, .13

No. 1466   3 inches . . . . Per foot, .11

No. 1459   3½ inches . . . . Per foot, .13

No. 1464   3 inches . . . . Per foot, .12

No. 1473   7 inches . . . . Per foot, .27

No. 1463   11 inches . . . . Per foot, .38

Deep and Bold.
No. 1423   10½ inches, exclusive of Flanges . . . . Per foot, .35

CURVED ENRICHMENTS

SCALE, 1½ Inches to 1 Foot

No. 2713   2 inches . . . . Per foot, $0.10

No. 2711   2½ inches . . . . Per foot, .12

No. 1632   3 inches . . . . Per foot, $0.18

No. 2712   2½ inches . . . . Per foot, .12

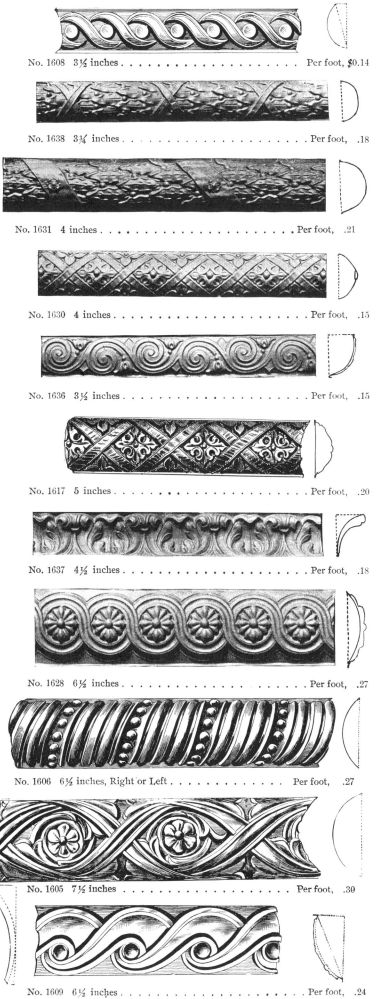

No. 2705	1⅝ inches	.	Per foot, $0.06
" 2703	1	"	.05
" 2704	1¼	"	.05
" 2706	2¼	"	.08
" 2707	3	"	.12
" 2708	4½	"	.21
" 2709	6	"	.27

No. 1608   3½ inches . . . . Per foot, $0.14

No. 1625	2¾ inches, exclusive of Flanges	.	Per foot,	.12
" 1619	2 " " "	.	" "	.09

No. 1638   3¾ inches . . . . Per foot,   .18

No. 1622   6 inches . . . . Per foot,   .21

No. 1631   4 inches . . . . Per foot,   .21

No. 2714   5 inches . . . . Per foot,   .24

No. 1630   4 inches . . . . Per foot,   .15

No. 1634   4½ inches . . . . Per foot,   .18

No. 1636   3½ inches . . . . Per foot,   .15

No. 1607   6 inches . . . . Per foot,   .21

No. 1617   5 inches . . . . Per foot,   .20

No. 1623   6 inches . . . . Per foot,   .21

No. 1637   4½ inches . . . . Per foot,   .18

No. 1628   6½ inches . . . . Per foot,   .27

No. 1612	8 inches, exclusive of Flanges	.	Per foot,	.30
" 1613	10 " " "	.	"	.38
" 1614	12 " " "	.	"	.45
" 1626	6 " " "	.	"	.23
" 1627	4 " " "	.	"	.18

No. 1606   6½ inches, Right or Left . . . . Per foot,   .27

No. 1605   7½ inches . . . . Per foot,   .30

No. 1624   8½ inches . . . . Per foot,   .30

No. 1609   6½ inches . . . . Per foot,   .24

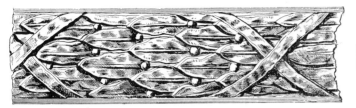

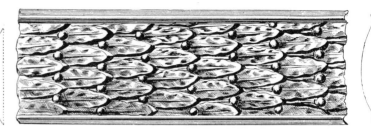

No. 1610   7½ inches . . . . Per foot, $0.30
"   1611   6½ "   . . . . "   .26

No. 1615   9½ inches . . . . Per foot, $0.33

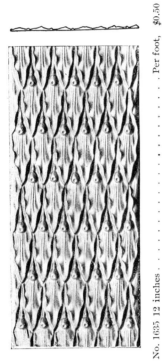

No. 1635 12 inches . . . . Per foot, $0.50

No. 1620   13 inches, very Deep and Bold . . . . Per foot, $0.45

No. 1629   16 inches . . . . Per foot, $0.60

BEAD ENRICHMENTS
SCALE, 1½ Inches to 1 Foot

No. 1945   ⅝ inch . . . . Per foot, $0.05

No. 1909   1½ inches . . . . Per foot, .08

No. 1941   1½ inches . . . . Per foot, .08
"   1942   1¼ " . . . . "   .07
"   1943   1 " . . . . "   .05
"   1917   ⅝ " . . . . "   .05

No. 1916   ¾ inch . . . . Per foot, .06

No. 1957   1⅛ inches . . . . Per foot, .07

No. 1959   1¼ inches . . . . Per foot, .07½

No. 1952   1⅜ inches . . . . Per foot, .08

No. 1960   1¼ inches . . . . Per foot, .7½

No. 1949   2 inches . . . . Per foot, .11

No. 1924   2 inches . . . . Per foot, $0.12

No. 1906   2¼ inches . . . . Per foot, .11

No. 1908   2 inches . . . . Per foot, .09
"   1925   1¼ " . . . . "   .08

No. 1905   2½ inches . . . . Per foot, .12
"   1910   1 " . . . . "   .07
"   1911   1¼ " . . . . "   .07
"   1920   ½ " . . . . "   .05
"   1947   1½ " . . . . "   .08
"   1946   2 " . . . . "   .10
"   1956   1¼ " . . . . "   .07

No. 1955   1¾ inches . . . . Per foot, .11

No. 1958   2¼ inches . . . . Per foot, .12

No. 1954   2⅜ inches . . . . Per foot, **.12**

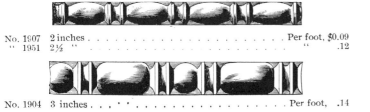

No. 1907 2 inches . . . . Per foot, $0.09
" 1951 2½ " . . . . " .12

No. 1961 6½ inches . . . . Per foot, $0.30

No. 1904 3 inches . . . . Per foot, .14

FRIEZE ENRICHMENTS

SCALE, 1½ Inches to 1 Foot

No. 2235 3½ inches . . . . Per foot, $0.12

No. 2236 3¼ inches . . . . Per foot, .12

No. 2233 4 inches . . . . Per foot, .14

No. 2226 12 inches . . . . Per foot, .42

No. 2603 6 inches . . . . Per foot, .20
" 2601 10 " . . . . " .35
" 2604 4 " . . . . " .15

No. 2210 6 inches . . . . Per foot, .20
" 2209 4 " . . . . " .14
" 2211 8 " . . . . " .27
" 2212 10 " . . . . " .33
" 2213 12 " . . . . " .38

No. 2611 16 inches . . . . Per foot, .55

No. 2602 8 inches . . . . Per foot, .27

No. 2610 14 inches . . . . Per foot, .45

No 2268 12 inches . . . . Per foot, .38
" 2289 18 " . . . . " .66

No. 2263 15 inches . . . . Per foot, .75

No. 2265   1 inch . . . . Per foot, $0.06

No. 2224   6 inches . . . . Per foot, .23
"   2223   8   "   . . . . " .30
"   2257   10   "   . . . . " .35

No. 2258   5¼ inches . . . . Per foot, .17

No. 2262   7 inches . . . . Per foot, .24

No. 2274   8 inches . . . . Per foot, .27

No. 2205   7 inches . . . . Per foot, .23
"   2202   4   "   . . . . " .14
"   2203   5   "   . . . . " .17
"   2204   6   "   . . . . " .20
"   2201   3   "   . . . . " .11
"   2206   8   "   . . . . " .27
"   2207   10   "   . . . . " .33
"   2208   12   "   . . . . " .38

No. 2266   7 inches . . . . Per foot, .24

No. 2243   6 inches . . . . Per foot, .20

No. 2260   4 inches . . . . Per foot, $0.12

No. 2261   4½ inches . . . . Per foot, 15

No. 2269   8 inches . . . . Per foot, 28

No. 2270   6 inches . . . . Per foot, .20

No. 2256   12 inches . . . . Per foot, .38

No. 2276   10 inches . . . . Per foot, .35

No. 2267   10 inches . . . . Per foot, **.33**

No. 2612   11 inches . . . . Per foot, $0.33

No. 2237   11 inches . . . . Per foot, $0.35

No. 2608   10 inches . . . . Per foot,   .33

No. 2216   10 inches, Right or Left . . . . Per foot,   .36

No. 2264   12 inches . . . . Per foot,   .64

No. 2250   12½ inches . . . . Per foot,   .42

No. 2215   9 inches . . . . Per foot,   .30

No. 2249   10 inches, very Deep and Bold . . .   . Per foot,   .40

No. 2244   30 inches . . . . Per foot, $2.70

No. 2271   15 inches . . . . Per foot, $0.50

No. 2278   15 inches . . . . Per foot, .50

No. 2279   17 inches . . . . Per foot, .60

No. 2248   18 inches . . . . Per foot, $0.75

No. 2219   18 inches . . . . Per foot, .75

No. 2245   18 inches . . . . Per foot, .66

No. 2222   13 inches . . . . Per foot, $0.42

No. 2247   14 inches . . . . Per foot,   .45

No. 2220   16 inches . . . . Per foot,   .60
"   2217   22   "   "   1.00

No. 2275   16½ inches . . . . Per foot,   .75

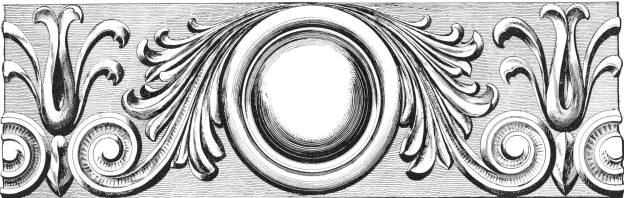

No. 2239   18 inches, very Deep and Bold . . . . Per foot,   .80

FLUTE ENRICHMENTS

SCALE, 1½ Inches to 1 Foot

No. 2841   1 inch . . . . Per foot, $0.08

No. 2839   2 inches . . . . Per foot, .12

No. 2820   3 inches . . . . Per foot, .15

No. 2823   2½ inches . . . . Per foot, .10

No. 2824   3½ inches . . . . Per foot, .15

No. 2827   4½ inches . . . . Per foot, .18

No. 2828   4 inches . . . . Per foot, .15

No. 2829   2½ inches . . . . Per foot, .12

No. 2831   2½ inches . . . . Per foot, .11

No. 2810   4   inches . . . . Per foot,   .14
"   2804   6⅝   "   . . . .   "   .22
"   2805   7   "   . . . .   "   .27
"   2807   5⅛   "   . . . .   "   .18
"   2813   2⅝   "   . . . .   "   .10
"   2814   2   "   . . . .   "   .07
"   2821   12   "   . . . .   "   .42

No. 2826   4 inches . . . . Per foot,   .18

No. 2825   4¼ inches . . . . Per foot, $0.18

No. 2809   5 inches . . . . Per foot,   .18

No. 2808   5 inches . . . . Per foot,   .18

No. 2802   9½ inches . . . . Per foot,   .33

No. 2815   8 inches . . . . Per foot,   .28

No. 2812   10¼ inches . . . . Per foot,   .33

No. 2822   7 inches . . . . Per foot,   .27

No. 2837   8 inches . . . . Per foot,   .30
"   2817   9   "   . . . .   "   .33

No. 2833   7¼ inches . . . . Per foot, $0.30

No. 2811   7¼ inches . . . . Per foot, .27

No. 2832   18 inches . . . . Per foot, .55

No. 2834   17 inches, Flange . . . . Per foot, .55

No. 2819   10 inches . . . . Per foot, $0.40

No. 2801   10½ inches . . . . Per foot, .38

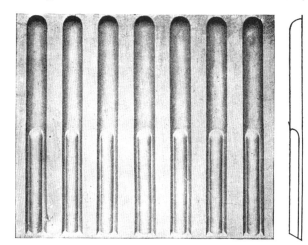

No. 2836   21½ inches . . . . Per foot, .70

No. 2818   12 inches . . . . Per foot, .42

PANEL ORNAMENTS

SCALE, 1½ Inches to 1 Foot

No.	Size.	Each.	No.	Size.	Each.	No.	Size.	Each.	No.	Size.	Each.	No.	Size.	Each.	No.	Size.	Each.
3413	3¾ x 4½ in.	$0.08	2418	5 x 5½ in.	$0.08	2445	5¼ x 4½ in.	$0.09	2440	7 x 7 in.	$0.11	2403	4¾ x 7¾ in.	$0.11	2404	6 x 7¾ in.	$0.11

LEADER STRAP.

No.	Size.	Each.	No.	Size.	Each.	No.	Size.	Each.	No.	Size.	Per Pair.	No.	Size.	Each.	No.	Size.	Each.
2464	8 x 5 in.	$0.12	3428	6 x 7¾ in.	$0.11	2422	6 x 8¼ in.	$0.14	2441	5 x 11 in.	$0.15	2407	7¾ x 9½ in.	$0.18	2466	7 x 7½ in.	$0.15
									2447	3¼ x 7¼ "	.09						
									2448	4¼ x 8½ "	.12						

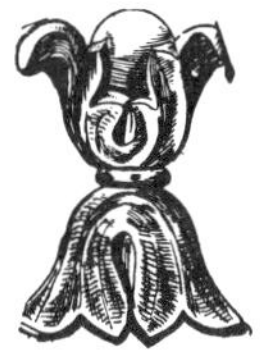

No.	Size.	Each.	No.	Size.	Each.	No.	Size.	Each.	No.	Size.	Each.	No.	Size.	Each.	No	Size.	Each
2401	2 x 4 in.	$0.06	2414	3½ x 4½ in.	$0.07	2444	5½ x 7 in.	$0.15	2479	7½ x 8 in.	$0.15	2408	8 x 9 in.	$0.33	2406	6 x 10 in.	$0.33

No.	Size.	Each.	No.	In parts.	Complete.
2478	6 x 8½ in.	$0.10	2467	$0.30	$0.50

ROUND LEADER STRAPS.

No.	Size.	Each.
2482	4 in.	$0.30

ROUND LEADER STRAPS.

No.	Size.	Each.
2468	5 in	$0.35
2486	6 "	.42

LEADER BAND ENDS.

No	Size.	Per pair.
2469	6 x 7 in.	$0.24

No.	Size.	Each.
2410	11¼ x 13 in.	$0.45

No.	Size.	Each.
2437	11 x 16 in.	$0.38

No.	Size.	Each.
2439	7½ x 12 in.	$0.23
2449	4¼ x 6¼ "	.09
2450	5½ x 8 "	.12
2451	6 x 9¼ "	.15

No.	Size.	Each.
2436	11½ x 16 in.	$0.42

No.	Size.	Each.
2435	10 x 16 in.	$0.30

No.	Size.	Each.
2432	8½ x 15½ in.	$0.30

No.	Size.	Each.
3426	9½ x 13 in.	$0.33

No.	Size.	Each.
2412	9 x 14 in.	$0.38

No.	Size.	Each
2472	11 x 12 in.	$0.40

No.	Size.	Each.
2429	21½ x 22½ in.	$0.68

No.	Size.	Each.
2453	8½ x 36 in.	$0.60

No.	Size.	Each.
2459	18 x 17½ in.	$0.85

No.	Size.	Each.	Mitre.
2474	16 x 18½ in.	$0.60.	5473
2475	12½ x 15 "	.50.	5472
2476	10½ x 12 "	.40.	5471
2477	8½ x 10 "	.30.	5470

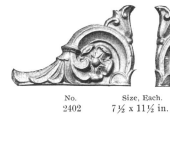

No.	Size, Each.	Per pair.
2402	7½ x 11½ in.	$0.45

No.	Size.	Each.
2416	17 x 20 in.	$0.65

No.	Size.	Each.
2415	15½ x 16½ in.	$0.90

No.	Size.	Each.
2481	15 x 27 in.	$1.00

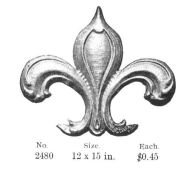

No.	Size.	Each.
2452	12 x 18 in.	$0.63

No.	Size.	Each.
2462	15 x 18 in.	$0.60

No.	Size.	Each.
2442	22 x 30 in.	$2.00

No.	Size.	Each.
2480	12 x 15 in.	$0.45

No.	Size.	Each.
2463	16 x 12 in.	$0.45

No.	Size.	Each.
2411	14 x 14¾ in.	$0.52

No.	Size.	Each.
2470	12½ x 26½ in.	$0.70

No.	Size.	Each.
2413	3 x 20½ x 10 in.	$0.55

TYMPANUMS AND PANELS

SCALE, 1½ Inches to 1 Foot

   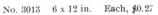

No. 3013 6 x 12 in. Each, $0.27   No. 3056 6 x 6 in. Per pair, $0.20   No. 3047 6 x 11 in. Each, $0.21   No. 3023 8 x 20 in. Each, $0.45

No. 3021 9 x 18 in. Each, $0.45   No. 3055 5¼ x 26½ in. Each, $0.45   No. 3009 10 x 22 in. Each, $0.60
" 3010 7 x 22 " " .45

No. 3007 26 ∷ 15 in. Each, $1.05

Very Deep and Bold.
No. 3608 19 x 19 in. Each, $1.05

No. 3046 12½ x 32 in. $2.40

No. 3048 10 x 29 in. Each, $1.00

No. 3002 20 x 12 in. Each, $0.75

No. 3057 18 x 37 in. Each, $2.50   No. 3058 18 x 30 in. Each, $2.15

No. 3049   14½ x 64½ in. $3.30

No. 3026	20 x 44 in.	Each, $2.40
" 3028	13 x 29 "	" .90
" 3029	17 x 37 "	" 1.60

No. 3027   12 x 36 inches, very Deep and Bold.   Each, $2.50

No. 3037   12 x 40½ in.   Each, $1.50

No. 3043   6 x 38 in.   Each, $0.60

No.	Size.	Each.
3014	8 x 72 in.	$3.00

These panels can be used in one foot lengths, separated at points 1, 2, 3, 4 and 5.

Any combination of these six parts can be made.

Each one foot section, $0.60

No. 3038   15 x 48 in.   Each, $1.80

No. 3045   12 x 20 in.   Each, $1.50

No. 3066   16 x 48 in.   Each, $3.75

No. 3039   10 x 36 in.   Each, $1.50

No. 3035   12 x 30 in.   Each, $1.00

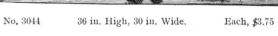

No. 3044   36 in. High, 30 in. Wide.   Each, $3.75

No. 3054   11½ x 33 in.   Each, $0.75

No. 3053   10¼ x 30 in.   Each, $0.60

No. 3052   8 x 24 in.   Each, $0.45

No. 3019   18 x 42 in.   Each, $2.25

No. 3061   22 x 54 in.   Each, $6.50

No. 3025   18 x 52 inches, very Deep and Bold.   Each, $4.50

No. 3024   18 x 40 inches, very Deep and Bold.   Each, $3.50

No. 3059   18 x 25 in.   Each, $1.80

No. 3020   18 x 60 in.   Each, $4.00

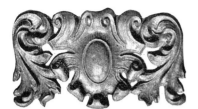

No. 3011   9 x 17 in.   Each, $0.50

No. 3050   12 x 21 in.   Each, $1.00

No. 3062   28 x 48 in.   In parts, $6.50

No. 3063   24 x 47 in.   In parts, $6.00

No. 3041   18 x 36 in. $2.10

No. 3005   21 x 18 in.   Each, $1.00

No. 3064   29 x 48 in.   Each, $6.00

No. 3022   11   x 24 in.   Each, $0.70
"   3031   15   x 33 "   "   1.20
"   3030   18¾ x 42 "   "   2.00
"   3032   22   x 48 "   "   2.75

Each, $14.00

30 x 108 in.

No. 3060

Each, $4.00

14 x 84 in.

No. 3001

No. 3004   8 x 26½ in.   Each, $0.60
"   3005   6 x 24 "   "   .45

No.   Size.   Each
3017   4 x 48 in. $0.75

No. 3051   13 x 72 in.   Each, $3.00

No. 3065   12½ x 54 in.   Each, $3.75

GARLANDS AND FESTOONS

SCALE, 1½ Inches to 1 Foot

No.			Each.
3265	18 x 7 in.	15½ in. centers.	$0.38
3266	22 x 7 "	19¾ " "	.45

No. 3246	8 in., wide.	Per foot, $0.30
" 3249	10 " "	" .35
" 3252	12 " "	" .40

No. 3206   2 ft. x 9 in. out to out, centers 21 inches,
Complete, $0.60
No. 3208   2 ft. 10 in. x 12 in. out to out, centers 30 inches,
Complete, $1.05

No. 3245	8 in., wide.	Per foot, $0.30
" 3248	10 " "	" .35
" 3251	12 " "	" .40

No. 3307   9 x 17½ in.   Each, $0.55

No. 3247	8 in. wide.	Per foot, $0.30
" 3250	10 " "	" .35
" 3253	12 " "	" .40

No. 3213   2 ft. 2 in. x 11 in. out to out, centers 1 ft. 10 in.
Complete, $1.00   -   In parts, $0.75

No. 3254   2 feet 6 inches x 7½ inches out to out, centers 2 feet 1 inch,
Complete, $0.95

No. 3216   1½ x 25½ x 3½ in.   Each, $0.27

No. 3257   1 x 30 x 5½ in.   Each, $0.36

No. 3243   Length, 2 ft. 2 in.   Each, $0.40
This can be bent to any curve, and with Ribbons, Drops and Rosettes, any
size Garland or Panel ornament can be constructed.

No. 3219   3 x 26½ x 4½ in.   Each, $0.30

No. 3237   3 ft. 4 in. x 9 in. out to out, centers 3 ft.   Complete, $1.00
" 3255   4 " 6 " x 12 "   "   "   4 "   "   1.90

No. 3242   3 ft. 2 in. x 12 in. out to out, centers 27 in.
Complete, $1.40 ; in parts, $1.00

No. 3220   3 ft. 2½ in. x 9 in. out to out, centers 2 ft. 2 in.
Complete, $0.90; in parts, $0.60

No. 3275   10 x 30 inches.   20 inches center. $0.90
" 3276   10 x 34   "   24   "   "   1.05
" 3277   10 x 39   "   30   "   "   1.20

No. 3258   3 ft. 6 in. x 15 in. out to out, centers, 2 ft. 6½ in.
Complete, $1.50 ; in parts, $1.20

No. 3269   2   x 27   x   5½ in.   Each, $0.33
" 3267   2   x 27½ x   4   "   "   .27
" 3268   3½ x 27   x   5¼ "   "   .36

No. 3408   3½ x 24½ in.   Each, $0.20
Can be used to form Wreaths.

No. 3203   7 in. wide.   Per foot, $0.28   11½ in. centers.
" 3201   7   "   "   "   .28   15½ "   "
" 3202   7   "   "   "   .28   19¾ "   "

No.	High.		Out to out.		Centers.	Each.
3295	5	x	27	x	24 in.	$0.45
3296	5	x	24	x	21 "	.40
3297	5	x	21	x	18 "	.35
3298	5	x	18	x	15 "	.30
3299	5	x	15	x	12 "	.26
3300	5	x	12	x	9 "	.22

No.	High.		Out to out.		Centers.	Each.
3303	7	x	21	x	18 in.	$0.40
3301	7	x	27	x	24 "	.50
3302	7	x	24	x	21 "	.45
3304	7	x	18	x	15 "	.36
3305	7	x	15	x	12 "	.32
3306	7	x	12	x	9 "	.28

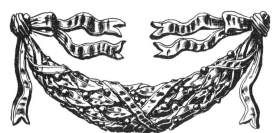

No. 3226   2 ft. x 10½ in. out to out, centers 1 ft. 7 in.
Complete, $0.90 ; in parts, $0.75

No. 3239   2 ft. 2 in. x 12 in. out to out, centers 2 ft.
Complete, $0.90
No. 3240   23 in. x 12 in. out to out, centers 1 6 in.
Complete, $0.75

No. 3210   2 ft. 10 in. x 17 in. out to out, centers, 2 ft. 5 in.
Complete, $1.60 ; in parts, $1.30

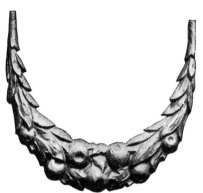

No. 3221   2 ft. 8 in. x 12½ in. out to out, centers, 2 ft. 5 in.
Complete, $1.15 ; in parts, $0.95

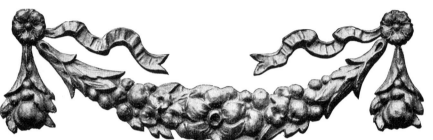

No. 3290	12 x 42 inches	36 in. center.	$1.35
" 3291	12 x 36 "	30 " "	1.20
" 3292	12 x 30 "	24 " "	1.00
" 3289	12 x 48 "	42 " "	1.50

Above Garland prices in parts.

No. 3204   16½ x 18 in.   Single Face, $0.75

No. 3212   3 ft. 7 in. x 14 in. out to out, centers, 2 ft. 8 in.   Complete, $2.00   In parts, $1.50

No. 3272   12 x 36 in.   Each, in parts, $2.00

No.	Size.			Centers.	Complete.	In parts.
3261	3 ft. 6 in.	x 9¼ in. out to out,		3 ft. 0 in.	$1.60	$1.45
3262	3 " 0 "	x 9¼ " "		2 " 6 "	1.45	1.25
3263	2 " 6 "	x 9¼ " "		2 " 0 "	1.25	1.05
3264	2 " 0 "	x 9¼ " "		1 " 6 "	1.10	.90

No. 3227   3 ft. x 14 in. out to out, centers, 2 ft. 8 in.
Complete, $1.75 ; in parts, $1.35
No. 3229   3 ft. 6 in. x 14 in. out to out, centers, 3 ft. 2 in.
Complete, $1.90 ; in parts, $1.50

No. 3205   8 x 17½ inches on center.   Each, $0.40   Per foot, $0.28

No. 3209   12½ x 23 in. $0.75

No. 3211   4 ft. x 15 in. out to out, centers. 43 in.   Complete, $2.00   In parts, $1.50

No. 3228   4 ft. x 22 in. out to out, centers, 3 ft.   Complete, $3.60   In parts, $3.00

No. 3217   20½ x 26 in.   Single face, $1.50

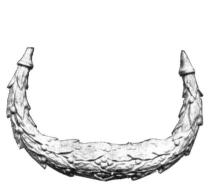

No. 3274   12½ x 19½ in.   Single face, $0.65

No. 3288	15 x 47 x 30 in. centers.	$2.10	No. 3283	18 x 47 x 30 in. centers.	$2.25
" 3287	15 x 53 x 36 " "	2.25	" 3282	18 x 53 x 36 " "	2.40
" 3286	15 x 58 x 42 " "	2.40	" 3281	18 x 58 x 42 " "	2.60
" 3285	15 x 64 x 48 " "	2.60	" 3280	18 x 64 x 48 " "	2.80
" 3284	15 x 70 x 54 " "	2.80	" 3279	18 x 70 x 54 " "	3.00

Above Garland prices in parts.

No. 3224   4 ft. 10 in. x 18 in. out to out, centers 4 ft. 2 in,   Complete, $3.00   In parts, each, $2.40
" 3223   4 "   x 18 "   "   " 3 " 5 "   2.40   "   " 1.80

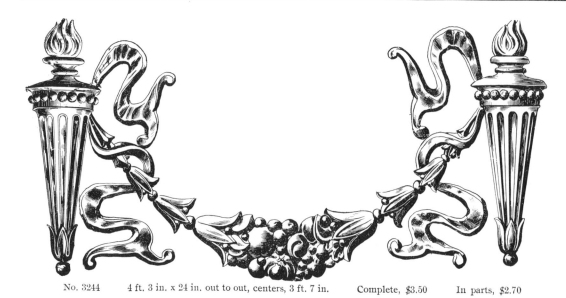

No. 3244   4 ft. 3 in. x 24 in. out to out, centers, 3 ft. 7 in.   Complete, $3.50   In parts, $2.70

No. 3271   36 x 54 in.   In parts, $10.50

GARLAND DROPS

SCALE, 1½ inches to 1 Foot

 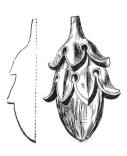  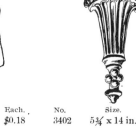 

No.	Size.	Each.	No.	Size.	Each.	No.	Size.	Each.	No.	Size.	Each.	No.	Size.	Each.
3403	7½ x 13¾ in.	$0.24	3424	7½ x 11½ in.	$0.27	2446	6½ x 14¾ in.	$0.30	3404	5 x 12 in	$0.18	3402	5¾ x 14 in.	$0.24

No. 3416
Size.   Each.
2¼ x 7½ in. $0.08

No. 3411
Size.   Each.
2¼ x 6 in. $0.08

No. 3412
Size.   Each.
2¼ x 8¼ in. $0.10

No. 3417
Size.   Each.
4 x 9 in. $0.11

No. 3406
Size.   Each.
3½ x 6½ in. $0.11

No. 3419
Size.   Each.
5 x 10¾ in. $0.18

No. 3418
Size.   Each.
4 x 9 in. $0.11

No. 3422
5½ x 12½ in.   .24

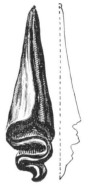
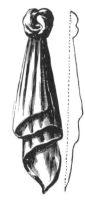

No. 3434
Size.   Each.
6 x 15 in. $0.26

No. 3432
Size.   Each.
5½ x 13½ in. $0.18

No. 3407
Size.   Each.
3½ x 10 in. $0.14

No. 3421
Size.   Each.
3 x 11 in. $0.12

No. 3405
Size.   Each.
5 x 16½ in. $0.24

No. 3423
Size.   Each.
5 x 17½ in. $0.30

No 2424   Size 11½ x 22½ in.   Each. $0.75

No. 3433   Size. 6 x 18 in.   Each. $0.30

No. 3409   Size. 8 x 27 in.   Each. $0.55

No. 3425   Size. 6 x 18 in.   Each. $0.30

No. 3427   Size. 7½ x 24 in.   Each. $0.45

RIBBONS

SCALE, 1½ Inches to 1 Foot

LEFT.   RIGHT.
No. 4001   2½ x 6½ in.   Per pair, $0.11

No. 4004   2¼ x 12½ in.   Each, $0.10

LEFT.   RIGHT.
No. 4044   3½ x 8½ in.   Per pair, $0.26

LEFT.   RIGHT.
No. 4034   6 x 6 in.   Per pair, $0.25

No. 4036   4 x 20 in.   Each, $0.28

LEFT.   RIGHT.
No. 4011   4½ x 10½ in.   Per pair, $0.18

LEFT.   RIGHT.
No. 4014   4½ x 12 in.   Per pair, $0.33

LEFT.   RIGHT.
No. 4015   5 x 16 in.   Per pair, $0.45

LEFT.   RIGHT.
No. 4007   6 x 13½ in.   Per pair, $0.45

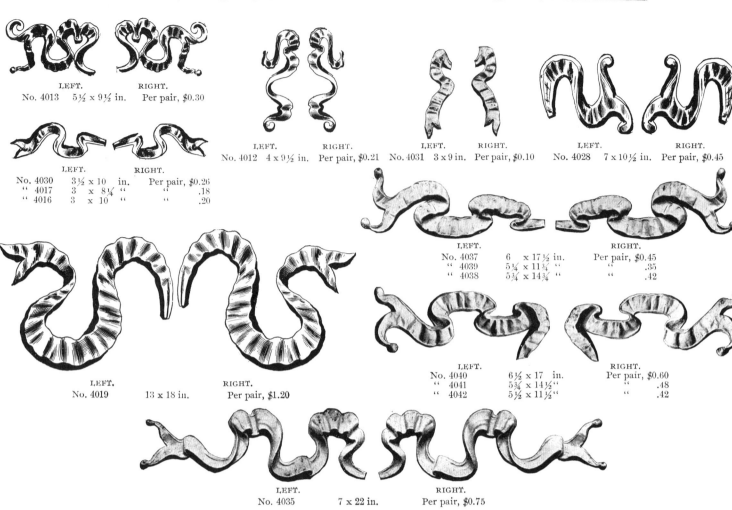

LEFT.   RIGHT.
No. 4013   5½ x 9½ in.   Per pair, $0.30

LEFT.   RIGHT.
No. 4030   3½ x 10 in.   Per pair, $0.26
"   4017   3 x 8¼ "   "   .18
"   4016   3 x 10 "   "   .20

LEFT.   RIGHT.
No. 4012   4 x 9½ in.   Per pair, $0.21

LEFT.   RIGHT.
No. 4031   3 x 9 in.   Per pair, $0.10

LEFT.   RIGHT.
No. 4028   7 x 10½ in.   Per pair, $0.45

LEFT.   RIGHT.
No. 4037   6 x 17½ in.   Per pair, $0.45
"   4039   5¼ x 11¾ "   "   .35
"   4038   5¾ x 14¾ "   "   .42

LEFT.   RIGHT.
No. 4019   13 x 18 in.   Per pair, $1.20

LEFT.   RIGHT.
No. 4040   6½ x 17 in.   Per pair, $0.60
"   4041   5¾ x 14½ "   "   .48
"   4042   5½ x 11½ "   "   .42

LEFT.   RIGHT.
No. 4035   7 x 22 in.   Per pair, $0.75

LEFT.   RIGHT.
No. 4002   5 x 24 in.   Per pair, $0.75

WREATHS

SCALE, 1½ Inches to 1 Foot

No. 4216   9 x 12 in.   Each, $0.30   No. 4217   7 x 8 in.   Each, $0.18   No. 4223   5 x 11¾ in.   Each, $0.22   No. 4214   9 x 9½ in. $0.41

No. 4225   20 x 24 in.   Each, $1.05   No. 4209   20 x 20 in. very Deep and Bold.   Each, $1.50   No. 4206   22 in. diam.   Each, $1.35

No. 4221   18 x 18 in.   Each, $1.25

No. 4227   17½ x 17½ in.   Each, $0.80

No. 4226   18 x 18 in.   Each, $1.15

No. 4222   12 x 15 in.   Each, $0.55

No. 4215   12 x 12 in.   Each, $0.38

No. 4202   16 in. diam.   Each, $0.70
"   4201   18   "   .85
"   4203   20   "   1.00

No. 4218   31 x 55 in.   Each, $3.00

No. 4212   12 in.   Each, $0.38

No. 4224   12 x 19 in.   Each, $0.55

No. 4220   18 x 20 in.   Each, $1.00

No. 4210   15 x 20 in. $0.60

BROSCHART & BRAUN : NEW YORK.

ROSETTES

SCALE, 1½ Inches to 1 Foot

No. 3769
2 in., each, .03

No. 3646
2 in., each, .04

No. 3791
2x2½ in., each, .03

No. 3645
2⅜ in., each, .04

No. 3833
2½ in., each, .04

No. 3656
2½x3½ in., each, .07

No. 3651
2¾ in., each, .05

No. 3654
3 in., each, .06

No. 3662
4 in., each, .09

No. 3658
3½ in., each, .05

No. 3755
3¾ in., each, .05

No. 3655
3¼ in., each, .05

No. 3827
3 in. each, .06

No. 3820
3 in., each, .05

No. 3760
3½ in., each, .06
No. 3859
6 in., each, .15

No. 3713
3 in., each, .08

No. 3712
3½ in., each, .11

No. 3657 3½ in., .07
No. 3650 2¾ " .05

No. 3661
4¼ in., each, .09

No. 3659
3½ in., each, .08

No. 3663
4 in., each, .08

No. 3667
4 in., each, .07

No. 3665
4½ in., each, .08

No. 3668
5 in., each, .10

No. Size. Each.
3795 1¾ in., .03
3796 2¼ " .04
3786 2¾ " .05
3785 3 " .06
3797 3½ " .07
3798 4 " .08

No. 3759
5 in., each, .10
No. 3860
10 in., each, 28

No. 3669
5⅜ in., each, .11

No. 3673
5¼ in., each, .12

No. 3674
5¾ in., each, .12

No. 3676
6 in, each, .13

No. 3681
6½ in., each, .15

No. 3678
6½ in., each, .15

No. 3680
7 in., each, .15

No. 3838
6½ in., each, .15

No. 3828
6½ in., each, .15

No. 3826
7 in., each, .15

No. Size. Each.
3753 7½ in., .15
3846 5½ " .12

 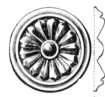 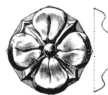   

No. 3818
7 in., each, .18

No. 3686
7¾ in., each, .18

No. 3685
8 in., each, .23

No. 3733
8 in., each. .23

No. 3756
7¾ in., each, .18

No. 3835
8 in., each, .18

    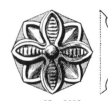

No. 3690
9 in., each, .32

No. 3840
9 in., each, 27

No. 3854
9 in., each, .22

No. 3836
8½ in., each, .20

No. 3682
8 in., each, .18

  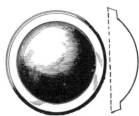 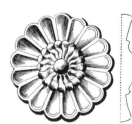 

No. 3688
8 in., each, .18

No. 3693
10 in., each, .27

No. 3729
10 in., each, .27

No. 3730
10 in., each, .30

No. 3694
10 in., each, .38

No. 3691
9¾ in., each, .32

No. 3824
12 in., each, .42

No. 3695
11 in., each, .38

No. 3814
12 in., each, .45

No. 3757
10 in., each, .39

No. 3845
12 in., each, .42

No. 3614
12 in., each, .45

No. 3726
12 in., each, .55

No. 3615
13½ in., each, .70

No. 3752
12 in., each, .45

No. 3697
12¼ in., each, .42

No. 3699
15 in., each, .65

No. 3849
12½ in., each, .50

No. 3700
16 in., each, .68

No. 3701
17 in., each, .85

No. 3746
16½ in., each, .92

No. 3703
18½ in., in parts, $1.05

No. 3856
18 in., each, $1.00

No. 3751   19½ in.,   each, $1.00
" 3847   16 "   "   .75

No. 3754   20 in.   Each, $1.25

No. 3750   20 in.   Each, $1.20

No. 3772   23 in.   In parts, Each, $2.25

No. 3771   22 in.   In parts, each, $2.50

No. 3761   15 inches.
Each, in parts, $0.85
Complete,   1.00

No. 3770   26 in.   In parts, each, 3.50   Complete, $5.00

No. 3803   18½ inches.
Each, in parts, $4.00   Complete, $6.00

No. 3767   30 inches   Complete, each, $7.50   In parts, $5.00

No. 6114   16 x 14 in.
Each, in parts, $1.60   Complete, $2.60

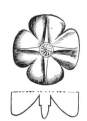

No. 3858 6½ inches.
Each, in parts, $0.25
Complete, .40

No. 3799 6 inches.
Each, in parts, $0.28
Complete, .45

No. 3800 3½ inches.
Each, in parts, $0.16
Complete, .30

No. 3782 5 inches.
Each, in parts, $0.25
Complete, .40

No. 3801 4 inches.
Each, in parts, $0.20
Complete, .35

No.	Size.	Each.
3762	6½ in.	$0.20
3765	4¼ "	.16

No. 3781 7¼ inches.
Each, in parts, $0.50
Complete, .80

No. 3823 8½ inches.
Each, in parts, $0.70
Complete, 1.05

No. 3776 8 inches.
Each, in parts, $0.45
Complete, .60

No. 3683 7½ inches.
Each, in parts, $0.40
Complete, .65

No. 3793 9½ inches.
Each, in parts, $0.40
Complete, .65

No. 3775 11 inches.
Each, in parts, $0.50
Complete, .70

No. 3778 13½ inches,
Each, in parts, $2.25
Complete, 3.00

No. 3802 13 inches.
Each. in parts, $2.00
Complete, 3.00

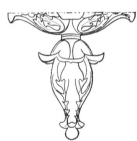
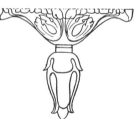

No. 3816 12½ x 12 in.
Each, in parts, $1.20
Complete, 2.00

No. 3815 13½ x 10 in.
Each, in parts, $1.05
Complete, 1.60

No. 3631
9 x 9 in. Each, $0.26

No. 3634
9 x 9 in. Each, $0.26

No. 3850 30 x 30 in. Each, in parts, $2.70 Complete, $3.50

No. 3842
8 x 8 in. Each, $0.22

No. 3632
8½ x 8½ in. Each, $0.27

No. 3617	No. 3837	No. 3619	No. 3603	No 3604	No. 3616
Size. Each.	Size. Each.	Size. Each.	Size. Each.	Size. Each.	Size. Each.
2¼ x 2¼ in. $0.04	2⅛ x 2⅛ in. $0.04	3½ x 3½ in. $0.07	5½ x 4½ in. $0.07	2½ x 4¼ in. $0.08	4 x 6 in. $0.09

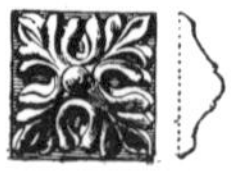

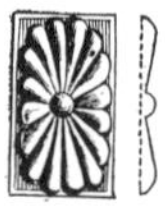

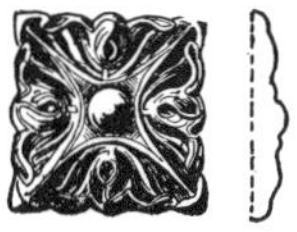 No. 3848	No. 3605	No. 3758	No.	Size.	Each.	No. 3819
5 x 5 in. Each, $0.08	4½ x 13¾ in. Each, $0.21	7¼ x 16 in. Each, $0.35	3621	6 x 6 in.	$0.1!	6 x 6 in. Each, $0.12
			3628	7¾ x 7¾ "	.18	

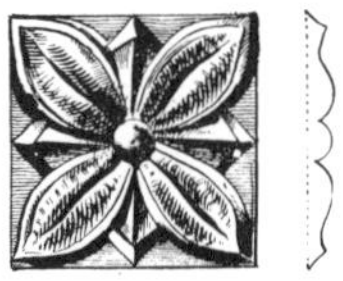

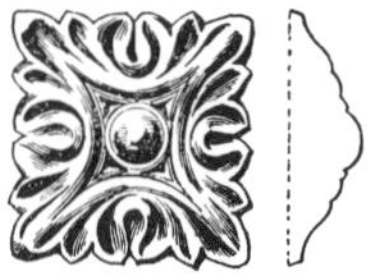

No. 3804	No. 3612	No. 3607	No.	Size.	Each.	No. 3626
6 x 6 in. Each, $0.12	8 x 12 in. Each, $0.30	6 x 7¾ in. Each, $0.15	3610	5 x 8¼ in.	$0.15	7¼ x 7¼ in. Each, $0.18
			3763	6 x 10 "	.21	

No.	Size.	Each.	No. 3633	No. 3851	No. 3602	No. 3613
3635	12 x 12 in.	$0.42	9 x 9 in. Each, $0.27	5 x 11½ in. Each, $0.20	8 x 10 in. Each, $0.21	10 x 12 in. Each, $0.36
3640	16 x 16 "	.60				

	No.	Size.	Each.		No. 3636	12 x 12 in.	Each, $0.45
No. 3825 15 x 15 in. Each, $0.60	3622	6 x 6 in.	$0.12	No. 3749 15 x 15 in. Each $0.60	" 3639	16 x 16 "	" .65
	3627	8 x 8 "	.18				
	3715	10 x 10 "	.30				

HEADS, EAGLES, ETC.
SCALE, 1½ Inches to 1 Foot

No. 4420 4 x 5½ in.	 No. 4421 3¾ x 4¾ in.	 No. 4466 5 x 5 x 3 in.	 No. 4416 5¼ x 5½ in.	No. 4422 3 x 4¼ in.	No. 4419 4¾ in.
Each, $0.20	Each, $0.25	Each, in parts $0.25	In parts, Each, $0.30 Complete, 0.50	Each, $0.15	Each, $0.25

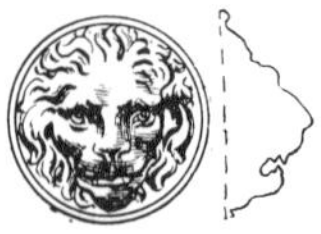

No. 4414 7½ x 7¾ in.	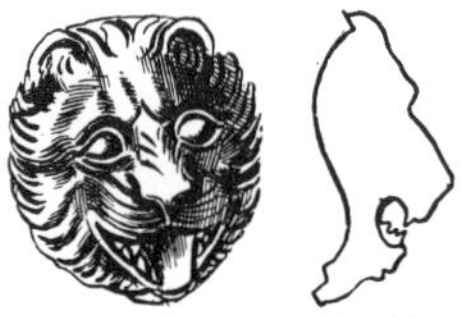 No. 4415 7 x 7¼ in.	 No. 4432 6¼ x 6¾ in.	No. 4453 9 x 10½ in.	No. 4411 9 x 9 in.
Each, $0.40	In parts, $0.75; Comp. $1.25	Each, $0.20	In parts, $0.50; Comp. $0.75	Each, $0.45

No. 4425   11½ x 12 in.
Each, $0.40

No. 4413   8½ x 9¾ in.
In parts, $1.00 Comp., $2.00

No. 4404.   8 x 10 in.
Complete, $1.80

No.	Proj.	High.	Wide.
4460	5 in.	8½ in.	9 in.

In parts, $0.90 Comp., $1.35

No.	Proj.	High.	Wide.
4458	5 in.	8 in.	8 in.

In parts, $0.90 Comp., $1.25

No.	Size.	In parts.	Comp.
4448	8 x 8 in.	$0.40	$0.70
4447	6 x 6 "	.25	.45
4449	10 x 10 "	.55	.90
4450	12 x 12 "	.75	1.00

No. 4409   11½ x 11½ in.
In parts, each, $1.15 ; Complete, $1.75

No. 4467   12 x 12 x 6 in.
In parts, $1.20 ; Complete, $2.00

No. 4408   12 x 13½ in.
In parts, each, $1.00 ; Comp., $1.50

No.	Spread.	Complete.
4451	18 in.	$4.25
4455	22 "	5.00
4456	19½ "	4.50
4418	16 "	3.75

No. 4407   14 x 15 in.
In parts, each, $2.00 ; Complete, $2.50

No. 4402   17½ x 21 in.   In parts, each, $3.00 ; Complete, $4.00

No. 4412   9 x 12½ in.
Complete, $2.25

No. 4470   14 x 18 x 7 in.   In parts, $1.80   Complete, $3.25

No. 4468   20 x 21 x 13 in.   In parts, $2.50 ; Complete, $4.00

No. 4429   12½ x 13 in.   Each, $0.75

No. 4431   16½ x 11½ in.   Each, $0.70

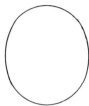

No.	Proj.	High.	Wide.	In parts.	Comp.
4475	8 in.	8 in.	6 in.	$0.45	$0.70

No. 4442   13¼ x 24½ in., full bodied, complete, $6.00

No.	Size.	Each.
4430	7 x 8 x 2½ in.	$0.40

LEFT.   No. 4443   13½ x 25½ in.   RIGHT. $3.00

No.
4434   19½ x 11 x 18 in. Complete, $10.00
In parts, $7.00

No. 4444   3 ft. spread.   Each, $10.00
" 4445   6 "   "   "   30.00

No. 4474   15 x 19 high. $2.10
Double Face.

No. 4454   In parts, $8.00   Complete, $12.00

No. 4457   36 in. spread.   27 in. high.
In parts, $18.00 ; complete, $28.00

No.	Projection.	High.	Wide.	Each.
4471	21 in.	36 in.	19 in.	$21.00
4472	30 "	48 "	24 "	28.00

No. 4473. Angle, 17x17x30 in.
In parts,   Each, $3.50
Complete,   5.00

No. 4463.   Spread of Antlers, 4 ft. x 8 in.
In parts,   Each, $25.00
Complete,   40.00

No. 4433
10½x14 in.,   Each, $1:20

SHIELDS AND CARTOUCHES
SCALE, 1½ inches to 1 Foot

No. 5114   22x24 in.,   Each, $1.50

No. 5116   16½x19 in.,   Each, $0.90
Very deep and bold.

No. 5113   19x21 in.,   Each, $1.10

No. 5112
7 x 7 in.   Each, $0.18

No. 5115
9 x 12 in.   Each, $0.38

No. 5130   24 x 46 in.   In parts, $3.00   Complete, $4.50

Very Deep and Bold.

No.	Size		Each.
5107	12 x 12	in.	$0.75
5106	9½ x 10	"	.40
5104	14¾ x 15½	"	.85
5109	16½ x 18	"	1.00
5119	5 x 5	"	.14

No. 5124
6 x 7½ in.   Each, $0.15

No. 5117   15 x 20 in.   Each, $0.90

No. 5127   15½ x 24 in.   Each, $1.25

No. 5108   14 x 16½ in.   Each, $0.60

No. 5123   No. 5131   No. 5102
10¼ x 11¾ in. Each, .40   6 x 8½ in. Each, .20   9½ x 10 in. Each, .36

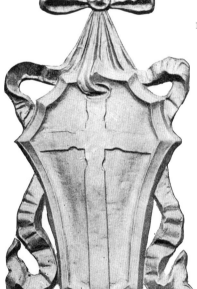

No. 5125   18 x 24 in.   Each, $1.50

No. 5129   12¾ x 24 in.   Each, $1.20

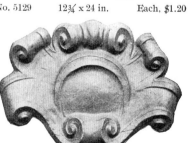

No. 5128   12½ x 18 in.   Each, .75

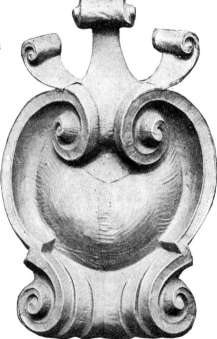

No. 5101   21 x 31 in.   In parts, $4.50
Complete, $7.00

SHELL ORNAMENTS

SCALE, 1½ Inches to 1 Foot.

No. 4649

6 x 7 in.   Each, $0.14

No. 4640

6 x 9 in.   Each, $0.18

No. 4647

6 x 9 in.   Each, $0.18

No. 4646

5¾ x 9 in.   Each, $0.20

No. 4639

5 x 8 in.   Each, $0.15

No.	Size.	Each.
4637	6 x 6 in.	$0.12
4634	10½ x 12½ "	.33
4635	8 x 8 "	.18
4636	7 x 7 "	.15
4638	5 x 5 "	.09
4633	4 x 4 "	.08

No. 4622

8 x 8¼ in.   Each, $0.15

No. 4620

12 x 12 in.   Each, $0.41

No. 4626

7¾ x 11½ in.   Each, $0.27

No. 4654

10 x 13 in.   Each, $0.45

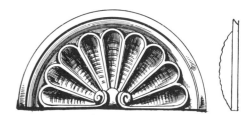

No. 4615   11 x 14½ in.   Each, $0.75

No. 4610   12 x 23½ in.   Each, $0.75

No. 4650   9 x 18½ in.   Each, $0.70

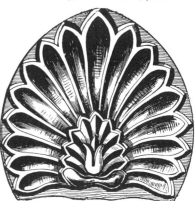

No. 4631   17½ x 18 in.   Each, $0.75
Angle Leaf for this, see No. 5427.

No. 4617   12½ x 22 in.   Each, $0.80

No. 4619   17½ x 18½ in.   Each, $0.75

No. 4616   11 x 15 in.   Each, $0.75

No. 4607   12 x 14½ in.   Each, $0.60

No. 4618   14 x 14½ in.   Each, $0.70

No. 4660   10½ x 12 in.   Each, $0.45

No. 4611   11 x 13 in.   Each, $0.60

No. 4656   8½ x 14½ in.   Each, $0.27
Mitre No. 5444

No. 4602   8½ x 10 in.   Each, $0.40

No. 4609

4 x 5½ in.   Each, $0.12

No. 4641

4¾ x 7 in.   Each, $0.14

No. 4661

5 x 8 in.   Each, $0.18

No. 4655

5¾ x 10¼ in.   Each, $0.22

No. 4605

5½ x 10½ in.   Each, $0.23

No. 4604   16 x 32 in. $1.50

No. 4603

7 x 9½ in.   Each, $0.28

No. 4658   11 x 16 in. $0.75

No. 4648   18 x 36 in.   Each, $2.00
Can be furnished in quarter, half or full circle.

No. 4606   15 x 20½ in. $0.75

No. 4612   13 x 34 in. $1.50

No. 4608   22 x 26½ in. $2.25

CAPITALS

SCALE, 1½ Inches to 1 Foot

No. 4884

✿ No. 4807

	No.	Height.	Abacus.	Neck.	Full Cap Complete.	Half Cap Complete.	Per Plate.
	4884	3 in.	5 in.	3 in.	$0.72	$0.48	$0.12
	4810	2 "	3 "	2 "	.60	.40	.10
	4812	4 "	6 "	4 "	.90	.60	.15
	4813	5 "	7½ "	5 "	1.08	.72	.18
	4816	6 "	9 "	6 "	1.50	1.00	.25
	4817	7 "	10½ "	7 "	2.10	1.40	.35
	4802	6 "	12 "	8 "	2.50	1.68	.42
	4820	10 "	15 "	10 "	3.00	2.00	.50
	4822	12 "	18 "	12 "	3.60	2.40	.60
	✿ 4807	4½ "	4 "	2 "	.75	.40	.10

All of same design as No. 4884

No. 4859

Height.	Abacus.	Dia. of Neck.
5¾ in.	6 in.	2½ in.

Full cap, complete, $0.75
Half cap,   "   .45
Per plate,   .12

No. 4869

Height.	Abacus.	Dia. of Neck.
6 in.	5¼ in.	2 in.

Full cap, complete, $0.75
Half cap,   "   .45
Per plate,   .12

No. 4829

Height.	Abacus.	Dia. of Neck.
8 in.	4½ in.	3 in.

Full cap, complete, $0.80
Half cap,   "   .50
Per plate,   .12

No. 4826

Height.	Abacus.	Dia. of Neck.
7 in.	7½ in.	4 in.

Full cap, complete,	$0.90
Half cap, "	.60
Per plate,	.15

No. 4882

Height.	Abacus.	Pilaster.
7 in.	8 in.	5 in.

Full cap, complete,	$1.35
Half cap, "	.75
Plate,	.18

No. 4804

Height.	Abacus.	Dia. of Neck.
6 in.	6½ in.	3 in.

Full cap, complete,	$0.90
Half cap, "	.60
Per plate,	.15

No. 4901

Height.	Abacus.	Dia. of Neck.
5¼ in.	4½ in.	2¼ in.

Full cap, complete,	.80
Half cap, "	.50
Per plate,	.12

No. 4847

Height.	Abacus.	Pilaster.
5¼ in.	8 in.	3 in.

Full cap, complete,	$1.00
Half cap, "	.60
Per plate,	.15

No. 4818

Height.	Abacus.	Pilaster.
6½ in.	9 in.	5 in.

Full cap, complete,	$1.30
Half cap, "	.80
Per plate,	.18

No. 4809

Height.	Abacus.	Dia. of Neck.
8 in.	9 in.	3 in.

Full cap, complete,	$1.50
Half cap, "	.95
Per plate,	.23

No. 4824

Height.	Abacus.	Pilaster.
4½ in.	9 in.	6 in.

Full cap, complete,	$1.00
Half cap, "	.60
Per plate,	.15

No. 4881

Height.	Abacus.	Pilaster.
5 in.	12 in.	8 in.

Full cap, complete,	$3.50
Half cap "	2.00
Quarters, in parts,	.60

No. 4880

Height.	Abacus.	Dia. of Neck.
5 in.	12 in.	8 in.

Full cap, complete,	$3.50
Half cap, "	2.00
Quarters, in parts,	.60

No. 4825

Height.	Abacus.	Dia. of Neck.
7½ in.	7¼ in.	4 in.

Full cap, complete,	$1.25
Half cap, "	.80
Per plate,	.20

No. 4827

No.	Height.		Abacus.		Pilaster	Complete. Full Cap	Complete. Half Cap	Plate.
4827	3	in.	5	in.	3 in.	$0.72	$0.48	$0.12
4830	4	"	6	"	4 "	0.90	.60	.15
4832	5	"	7½	"	5 "	1.10	.72	.18
4833	7	"	10½	"	7 "	2.10	1.40	.35
4885	6	"	9	"	8 "	2.50	1.68	.42
4834	10	"	15	"	10 "	3.00	2.00	.50
4888	12	"	18	"	12 "	3.60	2.40	.60
4893	2½	"	3¼	"	2 "	.60	.40	.10
✿4803	7	"	11	"	8 "	$1.80	$1.20	$0.30

All of same design as No. 4827

✿**No. 4803**

No. 4850

Height.	Abacus.	Pilaster.
7½ in.	12 in.	8 in.

Full cap, complete,	$1.80
Half cap, "	1.20
Per plate,	.30

No. 4863

Height.	Abacus.	Dia. of Neck.
8¼ in.	9 in.	6 in.

Complete,	$3.50
In parts,	2.10

No. 4864

Height.	Abacus.	Dia. of Neck.
8¾ in.	9 in.	5 in.

Complete,	$3.00
In parts,	1.80

No. 4838

Height.	Abacus.	Pilaster.
7 in.	11½ in.	7 in.

Full cap, complete,	$1.80
Half cap, "	1.20
Per plate,	.30

No. 4836

Height.	Abacus.	Pilaster.
9¼ in.	13 in.	7 in.

Full cap, complete,	$2.50
Half cap, "	1.60
Per plate,	.40

No. 4835

Height.	Abacus.	Pilaster.
12 in.	17 in.	10 in.

Full cap, complete,	$3.60
Half cap, "	2.40
Per plate,	.60

No. 4887

Height.	Abacus.	Pilaster.
11 in.	12½ in.	7 in.

Full cap, complete,	$2.50
Half cap, "	1.40
Per plate,	.40

No. 4849

Height.	Abacus.	Dia. of Neck.
11¼ in.	14 in.	8 in.

Full cap, complete,	$3.30
Half cap, "	2.20
Per plate,	.55

No. 4840

Height.	Abacus.	Dia. of Neck.
7¾ in.	9 in.	5 in.

Full cap, complete,	$1.59
Half cap, "	1.00
Per plate,	.25

No. 4811

Height.	Abacus.	Pilaster.
10 in.	10½ in.	6 in.

Full cap, complete,	$1.80
Half cap, "	1.20
Per plate,	.30

No. 4841

Height.	Abacus.	Dia. of Neck.
8¾ in.	10½ in.	6 in.

Full cap, complete,	$1.80
Half cap, "	1.20
Per plate,	.30

No. 4842

Height.	Abacus.	Dia. of Neck.
9¾ in.	12½ in.	7 in.

Full cap, complete,	$2.50
Half cap, "	1.60
Per plate,	.40

No. 4839

Height.	Abacus.	Pilaster.
9 in.	16 in.	9 in.

Full cap, complete,	$2.75
Half cap, "	1.80
Per plate,	.45

No. 4845

Height.	Abacus.	Pilaster.
11 in.	15 in.	8 in.

Full cap, complete,	$3.00
Half cap, "	2.00
Per plate,	.50

No. 4872

Height.	Abacus.	Pilaster.
6 in.	10½ in.	6 in.

Full cap, complete,	$1.50
Half cap, "	.75
Per plate,	.24

No. 4801

Height.	Abacus.	Dia. of Neck.
10 in.	10¼ in.	5½ in.

Full cap, complete,	$1.80
Half cap, "	1.20
Per plate,	.30

No. 4855

Height.	Abacus.	Pilaster.
9 in.	10 in.	6 in.

Full cap, complete,	$2.50
Half cap, "	1.20
Per plate,	.40

No. 4821

Height.	Abacus.	Pilaster.
15½ in.	21 in.	11½ in.
Full cap, complete,		$4.50
Half cap, "		3.00
Per plate,		.75

No. 4805

Height, 22¼ in.   Abacus, 25 in.   Dia. of Neck, 15 in.
Full cap, complete, $20.00 ; in parts, $12.00

No. 4843

Height.	Abacus.	Dia. of Neck.
15½ in.	15 in.	10 in.
Full cap, complete,		$4.50
Half cap, "		3.00
Per plate,		.75

No. 4867

Height.	Abacus.	Dia. of Neck.
14¼ in.	14 in.	10 in.
Full cap, complete,		$5.00
In parts,		3.00

No. 4868

Height.	Abacus.	Dia. of Neck.
15 in.	14 in.	9 in.
Complete,		$4.50
In parts,		2.75

No. 4870

Height, 22 in.   Abacus, 26 in.   Pilaster, 16 in.
Per quarter section, $2.25

No. 4871

Height, 22 in.   Abacus, 30 in.   Pilaster, 20 in.
Per quarter section, $3.00

No. 4851

Height.	Abacus.	Dia. of Neck.
9½ in.	11½ in.	8½ in.
Full cap, complete,		$2.20
Half cap, "		1.25
Per plate,		.35

No. 4865

Height	Abacus	Dia. of Neck.
11¼ in.	11 in.	8 in.

Complete, $4.50 ; in parts, $2.80

No. 4866

Height.	Abacus.	Dia. of Neck.
11¾ in.	11 in.	7 in.

Complete, $4.00; in parts, $2.40

No. 4878

Height.	Abacus.	Dia. of Neck.
12 in.	16 in.	12 in.
Full cap, complete,		$3.60
Half cap, "		1.80
Per plate,		.60

No. 4856.   Octagon

Height.	Abacus.	Pilaster.
9 in.	9 x 9 in.	6 x 6 in.

Per plate, $0.70,   with 2-in. Returns, $1.40
Full cap, complete, $2.75

No. 4806

Height.	Abacus.	Dia. of Neck.
16 in.	12 in.	6 in.
Full cap, complete,		$3.75
Half cap, "		1.80
Per plate,		.60

Very Bold Foliage.
No. 4848

Height, 21 in.   Abacus, 27 in.   Dia. of Neck, 14 in.
Full cap, complete, $20.00 ; half cap, $13.00

No. 4837

Height.	Abacus.	Pilaster.
10½ in.	16¼ in.	12 in.

Full cap, complete, $3.75;   Half cap, $2.40
Per plate, $0.60

No. 4814

Height.	Abacus.	Dia. of Neck.
13½ in.	14 in.	8 in.

Full cap, complete,	$3.00
Half cap, "	2.00
Per Plate,	.50

No. 4886

Height, 19 in.   Abacus, 32 in.   Dia. of Neck,18 in.
Full cap, complete, $12.00;   Half cap, $6.00;   Quarter section, $2.00

No. 4815

Height.	Abacus.	Dia. of Neck.
13½ in.	13½ in.	8 in.

Full cap, complete,	$3.50
Half cap, "	3.00
Per plate,	.75

No. 4819

Height.	Abacus.	Dia. of Neck.
12 in.	20½ in.	11½ in.

Full cap, complete, $4.50;   Half cap, $3.00
Per plate, $0.75

No. 4875

Height,	15½ in.	15½ in.	15½ in.	15½ in.
Abacus,	21 "	25 "	29 "	33 "
Pilaster,	16 "	20 "	24 "	28 "
Per plate,	$0.80	$1.10	$1.40	$1.70
	A	B	C	D

No. 4876

Height,	10 in.	10 in.	10 in.	10 in.
Abacus,	20½ "	23½ "	26½ "	29½ "
Pilaster,	16¾ "	19¾ "	22¾ "	25¾ "
Per plate,	$0.75	$0.95	$1.20	$1.45
	A	B	C	D

No. 4860

Height.	Abacus.	Dia. of Neck.
10 in.	12 in.	6 in.

Full cap, complete,	$3.00
Half cap, "	1.65
Per cap,	.45

No. 4862

Height.	Abacus.	Pilaster.
5½ in.	17 in.	9¼ in.

Complete, $6.00 ;   In parts, $3.90

No. 4909

Height.	Abacus.	Pilaster.
12 in.	18½ in.	9½ in.

Full cap, complete, $3.80;   Half cap, $2.00
Per plate, $0.66

No. 4896

OCTAGON.

Height.	Abacus.	Pilaster.
7 in.	9 in.	6 in.

Per double plates, $0.45

No. 4912

Height.	Abacus.	Dia. of Neck.
7 in.	10½ in.	6 in.

Full cap, complete,	$1.75
Half cap, "	.90
Per plate,	.30

No. 4906

Height.	Abacus.	Pilaster.
12½ in.	14 in.	8 in.

Full cap, complete,	$3.50
Half cap, "	1.80
Per plate,	.60

No. 4916

Height.	Abacus.	Dia. of Neck.
11 in.	12½ in.	8¾ in.

Per quarter section, $0.45

No. 4915

Height.	Abacus.	Dia. of Neck.
11 in.	15½ in.	10 in.

Per quarter section, $0.60

No. 4894   Height, 27 in.   Abacus, 30 in.   Dia. of Neck, 18 in.
Full cap, complete, $14.00   **Half cap, $6.75**   Quarter section, $2.25

No. 4900

Height.	Abacus.	Pilaster.
9 in.	13 in.	9 in.

Full cap, complete,	$2.75
Half cap, "	1.40
Per plate,	.45

No. 4910

Height.	Dia. of Neck.	Abacus.	Extreme.
14 in.	14 in.	18 in.	23 in.

Complete, $7.50 ; in parts, $4.50

No. 4892

Height.	Abacus.	Dia. of Neck.
23 in.	14 in.	10 in.

Complete, $6.30 ; per plate, $1.05

No. 4899

Height.	Abacus.	Pilaster.
9 in.	17 in.	12 in.

Full cap, complete, $3.25 ; Half cap, $1.65
Per plate, $0.55

No. 4913

Height.	Abacus.	Pilaster.
19 in.	36 in.	21 in.

Full cap, complete, $13.50 ; Half cap, 7.25
Per plate, $2.25

No. 4895

Height.	Abacus.	Pilaster.
6½ in.	10 in.	6 in.

Full cap, complete, $1.50
Half cap,   "   .70
Per plate,   .23

No. 4907

Height.	Abacus.	Dia. of Neck.
12 in.	13½ in.	8 in.

Full cap, complete, $3.60
Half cap,   "   1.80
Per plate,   .60

No. 4808

Height.	Abacus.	Pilaster.
7 in.	7 in.	4 in.

Full cap, complete, $0.90
Half cap,   "   .45
Per plate,   .15

No. 4911

Height.	Abacus.	Dia. of Neck.
3 in.	3½ in.	2¼ in.

Full cap, complete, $0.72
Half cap,   "   .36
Per plate,   .12

No. 4897
OCTAGON

Height.	Abacus.	Pilaster.
4½ in.	8 in.	6 in.

Per plate, $0.30

PINACLES, PENDANTS, WEATHER VANES, ETC.

SCALE, 1½ Inches to 1 Foot

No. 5064   3½ x 2 in.
Each, in parts, $0.15
Complete,   .25

No. 5065   4½ x 2½ in.
Each, in parts, $0.20
Complete,   .30

No.	Size.	In parts.	Complete.
6105	7 x 9 in.	$0.42	$0.65
5098	6 x 7 "	.24	.38
5099	10 x 12 "	.90	1.40
5100	8 x 10 "	.54	.85

No. 5026   8 x 9 in.
Each, in parts, $0.80
Complete,   1.50
No. 5025   13 x 14 in.
Each, in parts, $1.65
Complete,   2.45

No. 5094
6 x 8 in.   Double face.
In parts, $0.25
Complete,   .40

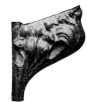

No. 5057   7 x 7½ in.
In parts, $0.45
Complete,   .70

No. 5075

No.	Size.	In parts.	Complete.
5075	7 x 4 in.	$0.45	$0.80
5076	8½ x 4½ "	.55	1.00
5077	9½ x 4½ "	.60	1.25
5078	10 x 6 "	.90	1.40

No. 5048   8 x 8 in.
In parts, $0.45
Complete,   .70

No. 5051   10 x 10 in.
In parts, $0.66
No. 5052   11 x 11 in.
In parts, $0.90

No. 5023

Height,	8¾ in.
Width,	6½ "
Return,	3¾ "

In parts, $0.30
Complete,   .50

No. 5083   6½ x 10½ in.
In parts, $0.60
Complete,   .90

No. 5024   6 x 10½ in.
In parts, $0.60
Complete,   .90

No. 5757   8½ x 11½ in.
In parts, $1.35
Complete,   2.20

No. 5062   13 x 9 in.
In parts, $0.85
Complete,   1.30

No. 5005
11 x 15½ x 7¾ in. Return.
In parts, $1.05
Complete,   1.60

No. 5073   7 x 9¾ in.
In parts, $0.75
Complete.   1.25

No. 5086   8 x 15 in.
In parts, $0.75
Complete,   1.15

No. 5047   23 x 17 in.
In parts, $3.00 ; complete, $4.50

No. 5762   18 x 12 in.
In parts, $3.00
Complete,   4.50

No. 5758   20 x 10½ in
In parts, $1.60
Complete,   2.50

No. 5046   22 x 18 in.
In parts, $3.00
Complete,   4.50

No. 5045   20½ x 33 in.
In parts, $4.50
Complete,   7.00

No. 6110   26½ x 32 in.
Per quarter section, $1.70

No. 5074   34 x 20 in.
In parts, $5.00 ; complete, $8.00

No. 5750   9 x 14 in.
In parts, $2.25
Complete,   3.50

No. 5004   10 x 18 in.
In parts, $1.80
Complete,   2.75

No. 5016   12 x 15 in.
Each, in parts, $1.80
Complete,   2.50

No. 5093   12 x 24 in.
In parts, $2.25 ; complete, $3.50

No. 6111   11 x 20 in.
In parts, $1.40
Complete,   2.20

No. 6107   3½ x 5½ in.
In parts, $0.20
Complete,   .35

No. 5082   2½ x 5½ in.
In parts, $0.18
Complete,   .30

No. 5092   4 x 4½ in.
In parts, $0.25
Complete,   .40
No. 6128   5 x 5½ in.
In parts, $0.30
Complete,   .50

No. 5080   4 x 4¾ in.
In parts, $0.20
Complete,   .35

No. 6115   5 x 6½ in.
In parts, $0.33
Complete,   .50

No. 5014   3½ x 6 in.
Each, in parts, $0.25
Complete,   .45

No. 5002   4½ x 7 in.
Each, in parts, $0.35
Complete,   .60

No. 5012   5½ x 8 in.
Each, in parts, $0.40
Complete,   .60

No. 5017   6½ x 6½ in.
Each, in parts, $0.45
Complete,   .70

No. 5015   5½ x 7 in.
Each, in parts, $0.40
Complete,   .60

No. 5007   5 x 9 in.
Each, in parts, $0.45
Complete,   .75

No. 5006   7 x 9 in.
Each, in parts, $0.60
Complete,   .90

No. 5089   9 x 10 in.
In parts, $0.90
Complete,   1.40

No. 5060   6½ x 10 in.
Each, in parts, $0.60
Complete,   1.00
Can be used for top on
No. 5061

No. 5011   7 x 14 in.
Each, in parts, $0.90
Complete,   1.50

No. 5084   6 x 14 in.
In parts, $0.65
Complete,   1.00

No. 5072   8½ x 11½ in.
In parts, $1.00
Complete,   1.50

No. 5008   7½ x 11½ in.
Each, in parts, $0.75
Complete,   1.15

No. 5001   9½ x 10 in.
Each, in parts, $0.90
Complete,   1.40

No. 5061   10 x 11 in
Each, in parts, $1.65
Complete,   2.10

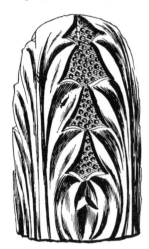

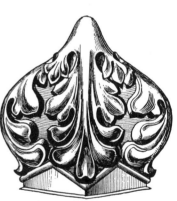

No. 5021   12½ x 21 in.
Each, in parts, $2.10
Complete,   3.00

No. 5729   Height, 18½ in.
In parts, $2.25
Complete,   2.75

No. 5096   17 x 20½ in.
In parts, $4.50
Complete,   6.75

No. 5707   Height, 16 in.
In parts, $2.00
Complete,   2.50

No. 5090   11 x 17 in.
In parts, $2.25
Complete,   3.50

No. 6112   12 x 22 in.
In parts, $2.10
Complete,   3.20

No. 5059   8 x 17 in.
Each, in parts, $1.20
Complete,   1.75
Can be used for top on No. 5061

No. 5029   16 x 16 in.
Per quarter section, $0.70
In parts,   2.70
Complete,   4.00

No. 6117   6½ x 16 in.
In parts, $1.20
Complete,   1.80

No. 5055   11½ x 19 in.
In parts, $2.10
Complete,   3.20

No. 6119
2½ x 4 in.
In parts, $0.15
Complete,   .30

No. 5095
5 x 6¼ in.
In parts, $0.38
Complete,   .60

No. 6103
3½ x 6¾ in.
In parts, $0.25
Complete,   .45

No. 5754
16 x 9½ in.
In parts, $0.90
Complete,   1.50

No. 6104
4 x 9½ in.
In parts, $0.45
Complete,   .70

No. 5003   4 x 6 in.
In parts, $0.30
Complete, .45

No. 6101
5 x 10 in.
In parts, $0.50
Complete,   .75

No. 6108   10 x 14½ in.
In parts, $1.50
Complete,   2.25

No. 5056
6 x 11 in.
In parts, $0.55
Complete,   .90

No. 5018
8½ x 9¼ in.
In parts, $0.90
Complete,   1.40

No. 5019
10¼ x 13½ in.
In parts, $1.50
Complete,   2.50

No. 5081   12 x 24 in.
In parts, $3.00
Complete,   4.50

No. 5752
5½ x 26 in.
In parts, $1.50
Complete,   2.40

No. 6116   12½ x 32 in.
In parts, $2.25
Complete,   3.75

No. 5744   25 x 10 in.
In parts, $3.30
Complete,   4.50

No. 5740   27 x 10 in.
In parts, $3.50
Complete,   5.00

No. 5035   8 x 23 in.
In parts, $2.50
Complete,   4.00

No. 5742   18 x 8 in.
In parts, $2.00
Complete,   3.00

No. 5724
Height, 2 ft. 3 in.
Complete, $3.75

No. 5743   23 x 10 in.
In parts, $2.30
Complete,   3.40

No. 5745   17 x 8½ in.
In parts, $2.00
Complete,   3.00

No. 5751   24 x 7 in.
In parts, $2.40
Complete,   3.65

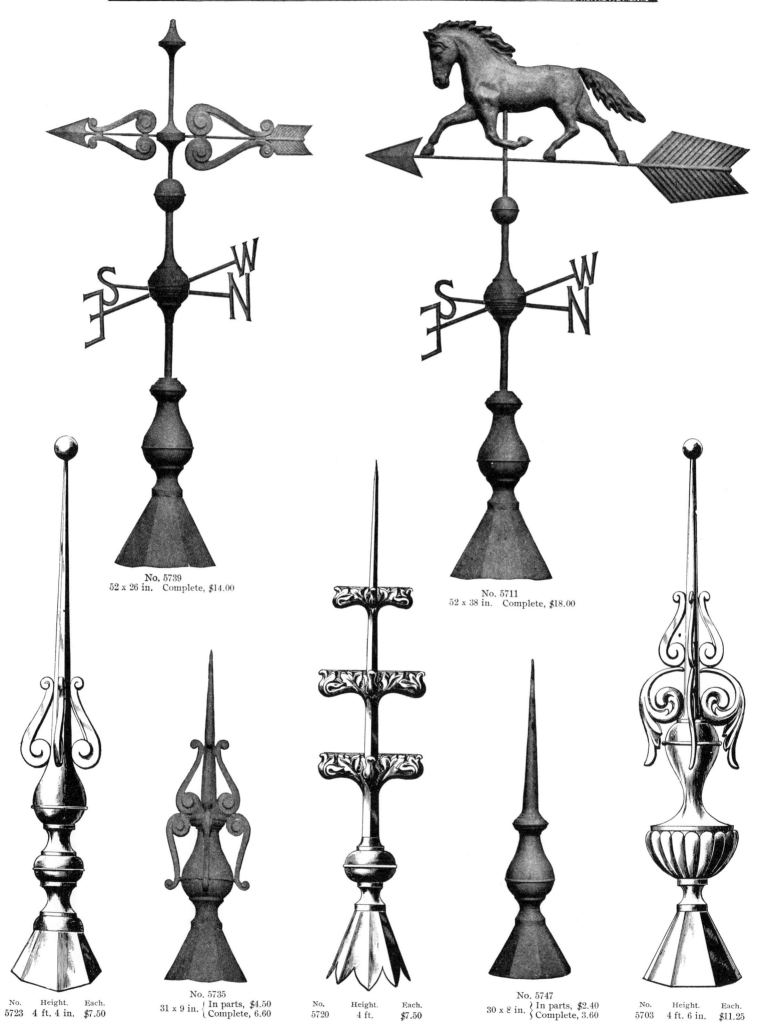

No. 5739
52 x 26 in. Complete, $14.00

No. 5711
52 x 38 in. Complete, $18.00

No.	Height.	Each.
5723	4 ft. 4 in.	$7.50

No. 5735
31 x 9 in. { In parts, $4.50
{ Complete, 6.60

No.	Height.	Each.
5720	4 ft.	$7.50

No. 5747
30 x 8 in. { In parts, $2.40
{ Complete, 3.60

No.	Height.	Each.
5703	4 ft. 6 in.	$11.25

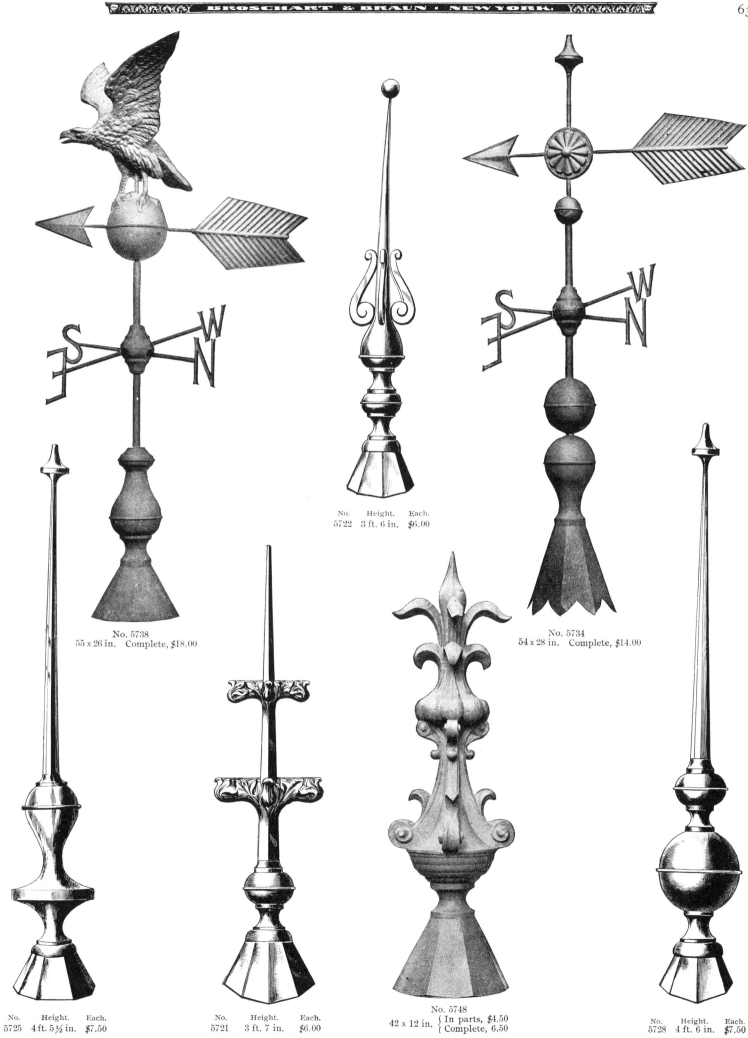

No. 5738
55 x 26 in.   Complete, $18.00

No.	Height.	Each.
5722	3 ft. 6 in.	$6.00

No. 5734
54 x 28 in.   Complete, $14.00

No.	Height.	Each.
5725	4 ft. 5½ in.	$7.50

No.	Height.	Each.
5721	3 ft. 7 in.	$6.00

No. 5748
42 x 12 in. { In parts, $4.50
            { Complete, 6.50

No.	Height.	Each.
5728	4 ft. 6 in.	$7.50

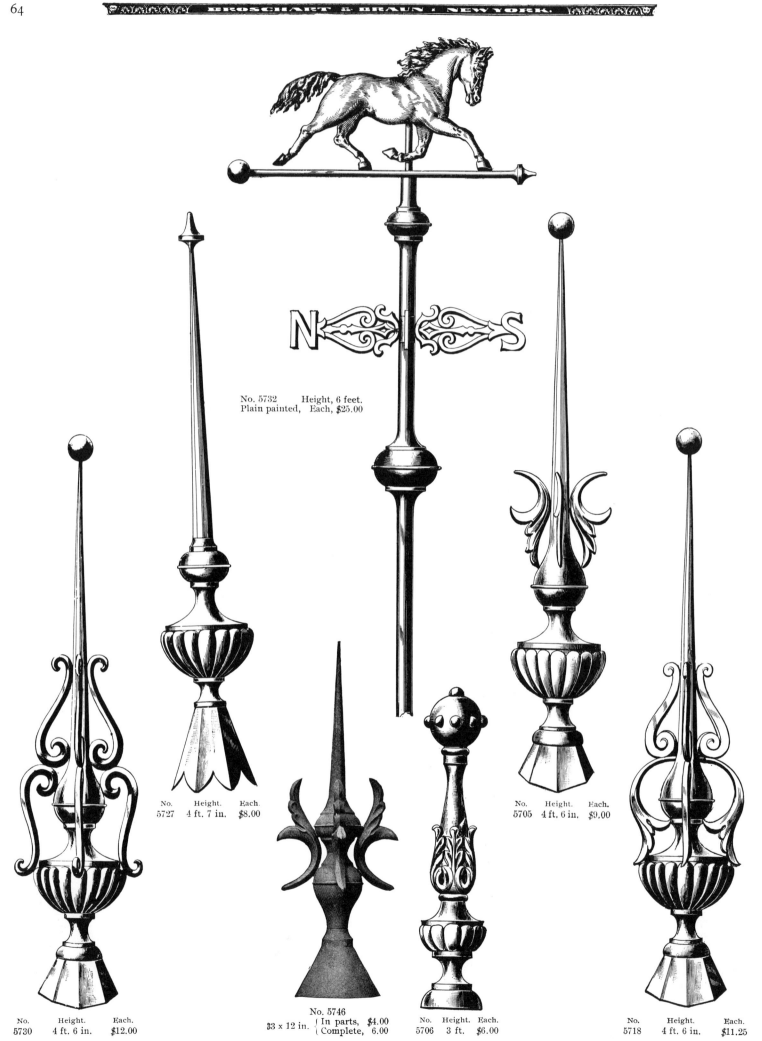

No. 5732   Height, 6 feet.
Plain painted,   Each, $25.00

No.	Height.	Each.
5727	4 ft. 7 in.	$8.00

No.	Height.	Each.
5705	4 ft. 6 in.	$9.00

No.	Height.	Each.
5730	4 ft. 6 in.	$12.00

No. 5746
33 x 12 in. { In parts, $4.00
{ Complete, 6.00

No.	Height.	Each.
5706	3 ft.	$6.00

No.	Height.	Each.
5718	4 ft. 6 in.	$11.25

No. 5733
51 x 24 in. Complete, $14.00

No. 5737
43 x 20 in. Complete, $12.00

No.	Height.	Each.
5701	4 ft. 10 in.	$11.25

No.	Height.	Each.
5726	4 ft. 5½ in.	$10.00

No.	Height.	Each.
5708	4 ft. 6 in.	$9.00

No. 5704
58 x 14 in. { In parts, $8.00
{ Complete, 12.50

BROSCHART & BRAUN : NEW YORK.

URNS

SCALE 1½ Inches to 1 Foot

No. 5043   9⅝ x 17 in.
In parts, $3.00
Complete,   4.50

No. 5741   19 x 9 in.
In parts, $2.50
Complete,   3.50

No. 5749   11 x 15 in.
In parts, $3.00
Complete,   4.50

No. 5710   9 x 21½ in.
In parts, $2.75
Complete,   3.75

No. 5755   27 x 10 in.
In parts, $3.00
Complete,   4.50

No. 5759   18¾ x 9¼ in.
In parts, $2.40
Complete,   3.50

No. 5763   39 x 16 in.
In parts, $4.50
Complete,   6.75

No. 5761   12½ x 5 in.
In parts, $1.20
Complete,   1.60

No. 5042   14 x 22 in.
Each, in parts, $4.50
Complete,   6.00
No. 5041   22 x 34 in.
Each, in parts, $6.00
Complete,   7.50

No. 6118   28 x 14½ in.
In parts, $4.10
Complete,   6.00

No. 5039   25 x 26 in.
In parts, $7.50
Complete,   11.00

No. 5044   33 x 20 in.
In parts, $6.50
Complete,   9.00

CRESTINGS AND CHENEAUS

SCALE, 1½ Inches to 1 Foot

No. 2255　　Drapery, 5 in.　　Per foot, $0.15

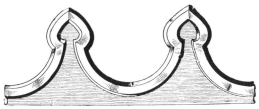

Single Face.
No. 5210　9 x 18 in.　Each, $0.45

Single Face.
No. 5212　12 in.　Per foot, $0.40

Single Face.
No. 5218　9¼ in.　Per foot, $0.38

Without Back — Very Deep and Bold.
No. 5209　13 in.　Per foot, $0.60

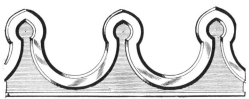

Single Face.
No, 5203　8½ in.　Per foot, $0.35

Without Back.
No. 5202　15 in.　Per foot, $0.45

Very Deep and Bold—With Back.
No. 5205　9½ in., with back, in parts.　Per foot, $0.70
"　5205　9½ "　Face only,　　"　　.45

Single Face.
No. 5204　15½ in.　Per foot, $0.55

Without Back.
No. 5215　21 in.　Per foot, $0.75

No. 5208　19½ in., without back, per foot, $0.90　　With back, per foot, $2.00

BROSCHART & BRAUN : NEW YORK.

No. 5234   3¾ in.   Per foot, $0.20

No. 5230   4½ in.   Per foot, $0.15

No. 5243   3½ in.   Per foot, $0.20

No. 5244   7 in.   Per foot, $0.24

No. 5240   10½ in.   Per foot, $0.60

No. 5232   8 in.   Per foot, $0.30

No. 5229   13 in.   Per foot, $0.60

Without Back.

No. 5201   18 in.   Per foot, $0.30

No. 5206   18 in., without back, in parts, per foot, $0.75 ;   with back, $1.60

NO. 5207   25 in., without back,   Per foot, $1.50

No. 5246   7 in.   Per foot, $0.27

No. 5238   9 in.   Per foot, $0.36

No. 5224   11½ in.   Per foot, $0.50

No. 5223   10½ in.   Per foot, $0.36

No. 5228   13 in.   Per foot, $0.55

No. 5237   16 in.   Per foot, $0.60

No. 5235   12 in.   Per foot, $0.40

No. 5226   15 in.   Per foot, $0.45

No. 5231   13 in.   Per foot, $0.45

No. 5219   19 in.   Per foot, $1.50

No. 5245   17 in.   Per foot, $1.00

No. 5233   24 in.   Per foot, $0.80

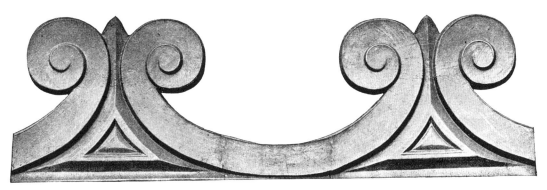

No. 5211   15 in.   Per foot, $0.50

No. 5222   20 in.   Per foot, $0.90

No. 5236   18 in.   Per foot, $0.75

No. 5239   19 in.   Per foot, $0.55

No. 5227   24 in.   Per foot, $3.00

No. 5214   18 in.   Per foot, $0.60

No. 5241   16 in.   Per foot, $1.00

MITRE LEAVES

SCALE, 1½ Inches to 1 Foot

No. 5426
Mitre for No. 4633
4 x 2½ x 2½ in.
In parts, $0.12

No. 5402
Mitre for E. & D.
No. 1164
In parts, $0.20

No. 5405
Mitre for No. 1478
6½ x 4 x 4 in.
In parts, $0.25

No. 5432
Mitre for E. & D.
No. 1161   7 x 6 x 6 in.
In parts, $0.30

No. 5401   3 x 8 in.
Per pair, comp. $0.25
In parts,   .18

No. 5461
7 x 17 in.   Per pair, in parts, $0.75
Volute for Cap.

No. 5412   13 x 5 x 5 in.
Mitre for No. 1635
In parts, $0.42

No.		Each.
5403	Angle Leaf, 4 in. Ogee Mldg	$0.09
5416	" No. 1429 & 1431 "	.21
5431	" 5 in. Ogee Mldg.	.15
5438	" No. 1453 "	.07
5437	" No. 1454 "	.07

No. 5443
4½ x 3½ x 3½ in.
Each, $0.15
No. 5491
3¼ x 2½ x 2½ in.
Each, $0.12

No. 5464
8 x 5 x 5 in.
Each, $0.30

No.					Each
5419 ·	Angle Leaf, 8 in.	Egg & Dart Mldg.			$0.30
5413	"	5 "	"	"	.15
5407	"	4 "	"	"	.12
5429	"	2¼ "	"	"	.07
5430	"	3 "	"	"	.09
5436	"	"	No. 1135 Moulding,		.09

No. 5444
8½ x 7 x 7 in.
In parts, $0.38

No. 5408   9 x 5 x 5 in.
Each, in parts, $0.36
Complete,   .55

No. 5424   8 x 10 in.
Each, in parts, $0.48
Complete,   .65

No. 5469   6 x 12 x 12 in.
Each, $0.50

No. 5439   11 x 7 x 7 in.
Each, in parts, $0.55
Complete,   .85

No. 5463   12½ x 12 x 12 in.
Each, $0.90

No. 5420   13 x 6 x 6 in.
Each, in parts, $0.80 ; complete, $1.00

No. 5472   12½ x 8 x 8 in.
Each, $0.54
No. 5470   8½ x 6 x 6 in.
Each, $0.30

No. 5425   13 x 8 x 8 in.
Each, in parts, $0.55
Complete,   .85

No. 5427   15½ x 10 x 10 in.
Each, in parts, $1.05
Complete,   1.30
Angle Leaf of No. 4631

No. 5445   18½ x 11 x 11 in.
Each, $1.15

No. 5442   19 x 9 x 9 in.
Each, $0.90

No. 5440   9 x 12 x 12 in.
In parts, $0.85
No. 5441   9 x 16 x 16 in.
In parts, $1.05

No. 5433   17 x 8½ x 8½ in.
In parts, $0.90 ; comp. $1.30
No. 5434   16 x 8½ x 8½ in.
In parts, $0.90 ; comp. $1.30

No. 5473   15¾ x 10 x 10 in.
Each, $0.75
No. 5471   10½ x 7 x 7 in.
Each, $0.40

SHINGLES, ROCK FACING AND LETTERS

SCALE, 1½ Inches to 1 Foot

No. 6303	12 in.	Each, $0.80		No. 6303	12 in.	Each, $0.80		No. 6305	10 in.	Each, $0.65		No. 6303	12 in.	Each, $0.80
" 6301	6 "	" .40		" 6301	6 "	" .40		" 6301	6 "	" .40		" 6301	6 "	" .40
" 6305	10 "	" .65		" 6305	10 "	" .65		" 6303	12 "	" .80		" 6305	10 "	" .65

No.	Size.	Each.
5933	3⅜ x 5 in.	$0.08
5932	3⅛ x 5 "	.07
5931	2½ x 5 "	.06
5930	2⅛ x 5 "	.05

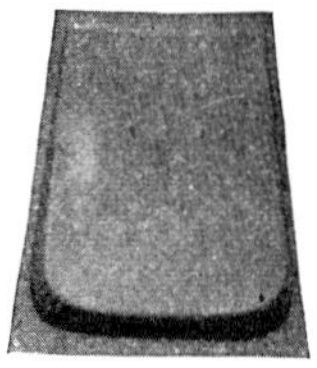

No.	Size.	Each.
5916	6¼ x 7 in.	$0.15
5917	4½ x 7 "	.12
5918	3¼ x 6½ "	.10
5919	2 x 5½ "	.08
5920	1⅜ x 6 "	.07

No. 6302	6 in.	Numbers.	Each, $0.40
" 6366	10 "	"	" .65
" 6304	12 "	"	" .80

No. 5921   7 x 11 in.   Each, $0.27

No.	Size.	Each.
5922	5¾ x 12¾ in.	$0.22
5923	4½ x 10½ "	.18
5934	4 x 9½ "	.15
5935	3 x 7 "	.12
5936	2¾ x 7½ "	.10

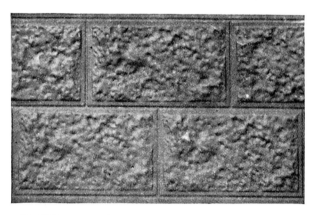

No. 5801   16 in. wide, Galv. Iron.   Per foot, $0.50

No. 5815   17½ in. wide, Galv. Iron.   Per foot, $0.50

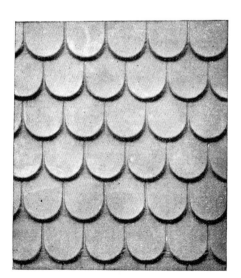

No. 5929   23 in. wide, 8 ft. lengths, Galv. Iron   Per foot, $0.60

No. 5914   23 in. wide, 8 ft. lengths, Galv. Iron   Per foot, $0.60

No. 5816   6½ in., Galv. Iron.   Per foot, $0.21

No. 5806   8 x 18 in., Galv. Iron.   Each, $0.45

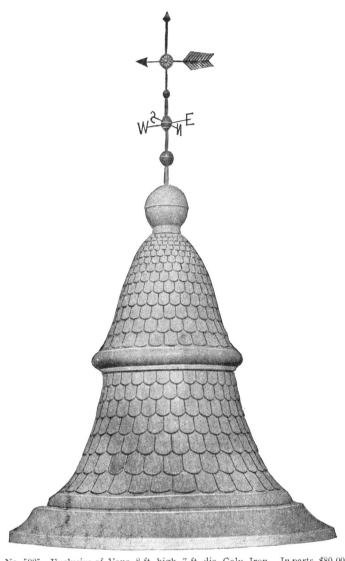

No. 5807   8 x 8 in., Galv. Iron.   Each, $0.24

No. 5925   Exclusive of Vane, 8 ft. high, 7 ft. dia. Galv. Iron.   In parts, $80.00
" 5925   Including Vane, 12 ft. high, 7 ft. dia. Galv. Iron.   "   130.0

BALUSTERS AND HALF BALLS
SCALE 1½ Inches, to 1 Foot

No. 6023   2½ x 10¾ in.
Each, $0.60

No. 6053   3½ x 12 in.
Each, $0.68

No.	Size.	Each.
6038	4 x 11 in.	$0.65
6029	3½ x 9⅜ "	.51

No. 6056   5 x 12½ in.
Each, $1.10

No. 6057   5¾ x 11 in.
Each, $1.15

No. 6026   6 x 15 in.
(Stamped)   Each, $1.35

No. 6061   5 x 13 in.
Each, $0.73

No. 6054   4 x 15 in.
Each, $0.90

No. 6024   5¾ x 12⅛ in.
Each, $1.65
No. 6075   6¾ x 16 in.
Each, $2.60

No. 6025   6 x 15 in.
(Stamped)   Each, $1.35

No. 6020
7 x 23 in. (stamped), Each, $2.75

No. 6062
6 x 17 in.   Each, $1.30

No. 6064
6 x 16½ in.   Each, $1.10

No. 6063
5½ x 18⅜ in.   Each, $1.45

No.	Size.	Each.
6045	6½ x 20	$1.70
6047	5½ x 15	.90
6049	5 x 13	.75
6037	4 x 10½	.60
6028	3½ x 8¾	.50
6072	5½ x 16	.95
6100	8 x 24	2.35
6097	7 x 22	1.80

No.	Size.	Each.
6042	4 x 20 in.	$1.10
6034	3½ x 17⅜ "	.90
6032	3½ x 15 "	.85
6041	4 x 19 "	1.05
6043	4 x 21 "	1.15

No. 6058
4 x 17 in. (stamped), Each, $0.90

No.	Size.	Each.
6050	5 x 18⅜ in.	$1.15
6039	4 x 16 "	.86

No. 6059
4 x 17 in.   Each, $1.10

No.	Size.	Each.
6044	4 x 21 in.	$1.20
6033	3½ x 16¼ "	.90
6035	3½ x 17⅝ "	.95

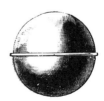

Zinc Half Balls, Butt Joint
1   inches, $0 75 per 100 Net.

1½	"	1.00	" "
2	"	1.65	" "
2½	"	1.90	" "
3	"	2.40	" "
3½	"	2.90	" "
4	"	4.10	" "
4½	"	4.60	" "
5	"	5.75	" "
5½	"	7.25	" "
6	"	8.25	" "

No.	Size.	Each.
6040	4 x 17⅛ in.	$0.96
6051	5 x 21⅝ "	1.20

No. 6019
3¾ x 15 in. (stamped), Each, $0.90

Zinc Half Balls, Bead Joint
5   inches, $5.75 per 100 Net.

5½	"	7.25	" "
6	"	8.25	" "
6½	"	9.00	" "
7	"	10.00	" "
7½	"	11.00	" "
8	"	12.25	" "
9	"	14.50	" "
10	"	17.75	" "
11	"	22.00	" "
12	"	29.75	" "
13	"	41.75	" "
14	"	49.25	" "
15	"	73.75	" "
16	"	79.75	" "
17	"	115.00	" "
18	"	143.00	" "

No. 6060
3½ x 17 in.   Each, $0.80

No.	Size.	Each.
6001	5 x 12 in.	$0.67
6002	4½ x 10 "	.56
6003	3½ x 8 "	.43
6004	5½ x 14 "	.80
6005	5½ x 15 "	.70
6006	5½ x 16 "	.92
6046	6⅛ x 18 "	1.50
6065	6 x 16 "	1.20
6098	7 x 22 "	1.72
6099	7 x 19¾ "	1.65
6902	8 x 22½ "	2.10
6901	8 x 24 "	2.15

No.	Size.	Each.
6011	5 x 20 in.	$1.17
6012	3½ x 16 "	.81
6013	4½ x 18 "	1.02
6014	5½ x 24 "	1.47

No.	Size.	Each.
6015	5 x 20 in.	$1.65
6073	5 x 18⅝ in.	1.35

No.	Size.	Each
6007	5½ x 16 in.	$1.00
6008	5 x 14 "	.85
6009	4½ x 12 "	.69
6010	3½ x 10 "	.57

No 6016
6 x 18 in.   Each, $1.25

No. 6018
5½ x 21 in.   Stamped.
Each, $2.40

No. 6017
6½ x 21½ in. square. Stamped.
Each, $2.40

[Original back cover]